# why do they do that?

**Practical advice to parents on how to tackle teen behavior**

# why do they do that?

*Practical advice to parents on how to tackle teen behavior*

# Nick Pollard
### with Eric Stanford

LION
PUBLISHING

Lion Publishing is an imprint of Chariot Victor Publishing
A division of Cook Communications, Colorado Springs, Colorado 80918
Cook Communications, Paris, Ontario
Kingsway Communications, Eastbourne, England

Cover and Interior Design: Big Cat Marketing Communications

First published in Great Britain. First American edition, 1999.
1 2 3 4 5 6 7 8 9 10 Printing/Year 03  02  01 00 99

                    **Library of Congress Cataloging-in-Publication Data**
Pollard, Nick.
        Why do they do that?/by Nick Pollard: adapted by Eric Stanford.
                    p.        cm.
        ISBN  0-7459-4087-0
            1. Parent and teenager.        2. Adolescent psychology.
3. Parenting.        I. Stanford, Eric.    II. Title.
HQ799.15.P65        1999                                99-31535
306.874–dc21                                            CIP

To the 6,000 or more teenagers who attend
my high school conferences each year and discuss
their beliefs and values with me so openly and honestly.
I hope that I may help you to explore spiritual
and moral issues. You certainly help me to gain some
insight into the impact of modern culture in your lives.

# Table of Contents

# Foreword

It has sometimes been said that a teenager living in New York City has more in common with a teenager living in a mud hut in an African village than he does with his own parents.

Whether or not that is strictly true, the fact remains that teenage culture is rapidly becoming globalized. That is why reprint rights on this book, which was originally written for parents of British teenagers, have been bought by publishers around the world—from Italy to Brazil. Most of the insights into teenage culture that Nick Pollard has discovered through his work with British teenagers are just as relevant to parents across the world, including us here in America.

However, no matter how much teenage culture is becoming globalized, there are still some differences. That is why I have added to this book many extra statistics and pieces of information drawn from our American situation. I have also changed some of the emphases and descriptions. For instance, in Britain most teenagers are professing atheists (in fact, a recent survey of 13,000 pupils ages thirteen to fifteen found that only 39 percent of them believe that God exists). In America the vast majority of teens profess a belief in God but are effective atheists, knowing little or nothing of a true relationship with the living God. Thus the terms that teenagers are using are different but the underlying fact is the same—as is the underlying cause-and-effect of such effective atheism.

What Nick and I have not done is to write an extra chapter about teenage violence. That is not such an issue in Britain as it is in America, and so it was not featured in the original book. However, it is a problem over here and does need to be addressed. Some of the reasons for teenage violance are in fact covered by Nick in this book when he looks at other issues. Teenage violence is due partly to the loss of self-control that he describes in chapter 5, partly to the loss of a respect for authority and the rule of law that he describes in chapter 6, and partly to the influence of Nietzsche (and that philosopher's emphasis on strength and power) that he describes in chapter 4. However, this in itself shows that the underlying reasons are complex and varied. That is why we have not squeezed it in as an extra chapter—it deserves a book all its own. Who knows? Perhaps one may be written in due course.


Eric Stanford
Colorado Springs, Colorado

# Introduction

*A thirteen-year-old girl is expelled from school for her abusive behavior and complete lack of respect for any authority.*

*An eighteen-year-old boy, known to be a regular user of ecstasy, is discovered unconscious in the restroom of a nightclub and dies on the way to the hospital.*

*A seventeen-year-old girl suffocates herself with a plastic bag, leaving a note to say that she cannot face taking her exams.*

Almost every day the newspapers report yet more tragedies that teenagers have inflicted upon themselves or upon other people. For many of us these are not just abstract stories in the press. We see similar disasters just waiting to happen in the lives of our own children or those of friends or those we teach. Every time we hear of a young person who has started sniffing glue or taken to the streets or become anorexic, many of us ask the same question: "Why do they do that?"

Why do they criticize everything? Why do they take drugs? Why don't they respect authority? Why do they develop eating disorders? Why are they obsessed with fitting an image? Why are they so sexually promiscuous? Why don't they see the value of old people? Why don't they get up and do something useful? Why? Why? Why?

For many of us, teenagers can be a real mystery. It's as if they have come from another planet. Parents, in particular, can find it hard to understand them, let alone be held responsible for their actions. We may be tempted to take the advice of Mark Twain, who recommended that when a boy gets to be thirteen years old he should be sealed in a barrel with just a small hole for air. And then when he reaches fifteen the hole should be bunged up.

Through my work with teenagers over the past ten years, I have met many parents who feel that they have failed. They have often come to me in tears, asking, "What have I done wrong?" They describe the behavior of their son or daughter and then say, "It must be our fault." This book is written for all those parents who feel like this. I hope that, after reading it, you will find those feelings of guilt and failure lifting from your shoulders.

Of course, there are things that parents can do to relate better to their teenage children and to help them more effectively. We will look at some of these at the end of each chapter. But before we can consider how we might respond to any particular teenage behavior in any particular situation, we must obtain a general understanding of why it is that so many teenagers behave in the way they do. We can't think about particular solutions until we have understood the underlying causes. So the beginning of each of the six chapters of this book will look at a different feature of teenage behavior and examine the fundamental causes that lie behind it. We will then see that many of these root causes lie not so much in the home or in the parents but rather in the massive shifts that have taken place in Western culture in recent years.

It is because these root causes lie in the culture and not the home that I feel able to write this book. I am not a parent of teenage children, nor have I ever been (although I will be in the future). However, I have spent the past ten years working, and practically living, in teenage culture. And I continue to do so. It was through this work that I began to gain an insight into some of the underlying causes of certain forms of teenage behavior.

I then discovered that many parents found their teenage children apparently impossible to comprehend because they didn't understand these root causes. Whenever I was able to help them gain an insight into the culture in which their teenagers were growing up, I noticed their faces transform. Now they could see why their teenagers behaved in this way—and they were able to think clearly about what they should do. Having seen this response in so many parents, I was delighted to be asked to write this book.

This, then, is not a book about parenting teenagers so much as a book about understanding the culture in which teenagers live. But I have no doubt you will find that, as you begin to understand this culture better, you will be able to understand your particular teenagers better, and then to help them more effectively.

## Things Aren't What They Used to Be

The term "teenager" was coined in 1942 by market researchers who were looking for a new category of young people to whom they could target their goods. Since then a lot has changed.

At that time, if you asked a teenage boy what he most wanted, he would probably say, "A suit just like my dad's." Today that's the last thing he wants!

According to the California Police Department and the Department of Education in Fullerton, California, the top seven discipline problems in schools in 1940 were talking in class, chewing gum, getting out of line, running in the halls, making noise, wearing improper clothes, and not putting trash in the wastepaper basket. However, in 1990 the top seven problems had become drug abuse, alcohol abuse, pregnancy, rape, suicide, robbery, and assault.

There is no doubt that teenagers are very different today. And so is the world in which they live. Our culture has gone through massive changes in the last few decades—at a depth, a scale, and a pace that have never before been known in the history of civilization. Unless we are aware of these changes and have thought through their implications, we will not be able to understand the teenagers who are growing up among them. Nor will we even begin to have any answer to that constant question "Why do they do that?"

Douglas Rushkoff, the American journalist and social

commentator, said in his recent book, "Our world is changing so rapidly that we can hardly track the differences, much less cope with them. Whether it's call-waiting, MTV, digital cash, or fuzzy logic, we are bombarded every day with an increasing number of words, devices, ideas, and events that we do not understand. On a large scale, the cultural institutions on which we have grown dependent—organized religion, our leaders and heroes, the medical establishment, corporate employers, even nation states and the family itself—appear to have crumbled under their own weight, and all within the same few decades. Without having migrated an inch we have nonetheless traveled further than any generation in history."[1]

We must wake up to the fact that we are in uncharted waters. Never before in the history of civilization has a generation grown up among such extensive cultural change. During the last few decades, almost all of Western culture's underlying beliefs and values have been turned upside down. Philosophically, we have shifted from modernism to postmodernism (don't worry, this will be explained later!). Educationally, we have moved from a didactic to a critical teaching model (and this!). Sociologically, many of our communities and families have disintegrated. Psychologically, new ways of viewing brain function have destroyed the previously foundational concepts of our individual identity. Politically, the fall of communism has rewritten the world map. Economically, the triumph of individual consumerism over socialism has changed the way in which we determine value. Medically, previously impossible treatments have become commonplace and expected. Technologically, computers and the

Internet have offered us instant access to information throughout the world. And the list goes on.

Wherever we look in Western culture there have been massive changes during the last few decades. Should we be surprised, then, when those of us who grew up before those changes took hold find it hard to understand those who are growing up knowing only a world full of such changes?

Clearly it is inevitable that we should be puzzled by teenage behavior. Teenagers are so different from the way we were at their age because the world in which they are growing up is so different from the world we knew even as little as twenty or thirty years ago.

And yet this is the world that we all know today. There are certain aspects of teenage culture that are unique to teenagers, but much of teenage culture is shared with the wider culture in which we all live. Indeed, most of the influential cultural changes we will consider in this book are general cultural changes and are not limited to the teenage subculture. Here, then, lies a curious paradox. We find it hard to understand teenagers because we don't understand the world in which they are growing up—and yet that world is the same world in which we ourselves live right now. It is not the world in which we grew up; it is not the world that shaped us through our formative years; but it is the world in which we live today. So why, then, don't we understand it?

Perhaps the answer to that paradox lies in an old Chinese proverb, which says, "If you want to know what water is like, don't ask a fish." The more we are surrounded by something, the less we are aware of it. We can become so familiar with things around us that we don't really think about them at all. When I travel in America, people sometimes say to me, "Gee, I love your accent." That always takes me by surprise because I don't think I have an accent. They are the ones who have the accent. I just talk normally. But of course I do have an accent, only I am so used to it that I am not aware of it.

In the same way, although we live in this world, many of us do not have a clear insight into it. In any case, most of us are so busy surviving that we don't have the time to reflect upon the underlying nature of our culture. But we must do so. We must become aware of our social and philosophical "accents" because it is only when we understand our world at this deeper level that we will be able to respond to the issues we face on the surface.

I hope that as you read this book you will be able to take time to think about the world in which we live, in particular to consider the effect that the massive cultural changes of the last few decades have had upon today's teenagers. Only when we understand why teenagers behave in the way they do will we be able to think clearly about how things might be different. Although we may not be individually responsible for the shifts that have taken place in our world, perhaps together we can do something about them.

That is why each chapter contains suggestions not only as to what we might do on an individual and family basis but also as to things we might call for in society at large. If our changed culture is having such a devastating effect upon today's teenagers, then, for the sake of tomorrow's teenagers we must see our culture change again—not necessarily back to how it was, but perhaps onward to something far better.

Some of the underlying concepts examined in the chapters ahead will take some effort to understand. They are not all easy, but they are all vital. It is always less difficult to look at just the surface of things, but that is not usually where the real answers are to be found. Indeed, simple, superficial answers can mislead us terribly.

The writer and commentator Os Guinness used to tell a story about a security guard at a Russian factory. One day this guard stopped a worker who was walking out of the factory gate, pushing a wheelbarrow with a suspicious—looking package in it. The guard opened up the package to find that it contained nothing but some old bits of rubbish, sawdust, and sweepings from the floor. The next day he stopped the same worker, who was again pushing a wheelbarrow containing a suspicious—looking package. Once more it contained nothing of value. After the same thing had happened many days in succession, the guard finally said to the worker, "OK, I give up. I know you must be up to something, but I don't know what it is. I promise I won't arrest you. But please put me out of my misery. Tell me what you are stealing." The worker looked at the guard and smiled as he replied, "Wheelbarrows, my friend. I'm stealing wheelbarrows."

Rather like that guard, we can spend our time looking at the surface of things and miss the real answers that might be found if only we would look and think deeply enough. So let's try to get below the surface. Let's probe into our culture and try to analyze it. Let's be prepared to look back in history. Let's be willing to think about underlying philosophies. Let's do whatever it takes to answer the question "Why do they do that?"

# "All You Ever Do Is Criticize"
## *Understanding Teen Cynicism*

*"You can always tell a teenager ... but you can't tell him much."*
*—a car bumper sticker*

*"Employ a teenager ... while he still knows everything."*
*—another car bumper sticker*

"I'm at the end of my tether," Cathy[1] said as she came into my room. "Why do my kids have to be so critical all the time? They simply won't accept anything I say. They have always got to question it and criticize it. They used to be so nice and easygoing, but since they became teenagers, they have turned into a bunch of cynics."

Cathy has three teenage children. They are all getting

on well at school. They do their fair share of messing around and they usually leave their homework to the last minute, but they work hard when they have to, they pass their exams, and they have a good group of friends. They are not part of a difficult or disruptive minority. In fact, they are average teenagers. And like many teenagers, they have a tendency to criticize everything and have become cynical about many things.

Cathy is an intelligent woman, a former teacher. But she clearly had no idea why her children had become so critical. She thought that, in some way, it must be her fault—she must have brought them up badly. When she came to see me, she was convinced that as a parent she was a dismal failure.

I made Cathy a cup of tea and sat her down in a chair. I then spent the next quarter of an hour explaining to her the educational changes that have taken place in our schools over the past few decades and the philosophical changes that have taken place in the wider culture during the same period. At first she couldn't believe how any of this would help her with the problem she faced with her teenagers. She clearly thought the consultation was going to have about as much relevance as learning the finer points of Vietnamese glassblowing.

But then, suddenly, her face lightened. She looked up with a smile. "Now I see," she said. "Of course, I should have realized. I saw these changes begin when I was still teaching. But I didn't realize how much effect they would have upon today's teenagers."

Cathy had just had what psychologists call an "aha experience." This is a situation where people say, "Aha! Now I understand." For Cathy, the light had dawned. I hadn't given her a set of quick, superficial tips on parenting teenagers. She didn't need that. But I had helped her to see some of the root causes underlying her teenage children's behavior. We then were able to spend the next half hour thinking through specific ways in which she could help them from now on.

Many of us are like Cathy. We look at critical, even cynical, teenagers and ask ourselves, Why do they do that? So let's try to answer that question by considering the underlying causes that I explained to Cathy that afternoon. Let's look at some educational theory and then some philosophy. You might think, as Cathy did at first, that these can't be relevant, but please stick with me and wait for the "aha experience."

## A Shift in Education Leads to Criticism

Over the last few decades a major shift has taken place in the educational model that many schools use. Many educational establishments have changed from teaching according to the "didactic model" to using the "critical method," at least by some teachers in some subjects.

The application of the didactic model in education is sometimes referred to as "teacher—centered teaching." This assumes that education is a process through which knowledge that is held by the teacher is passed on to the pupil. When a school follows this model of education, the teacher speaks while the students listen. To facilitate this, the classroom is set up with rows of desks at which the pupils all sit still, facing the teacher, listening carefully, and taking appropriate notes.

This was the style of education that I experienced throughout my time at school in the 1960s and early

1970s. Whether I was learning history, physics, or geography, I was taught a body of knowledge by the teachers, which I was then expected to learn and to reproduce in regular tests and examinations. Through this educational model I was taught a set of answers and was later given a set of questions. However, when I arrived at my university a few years later, I was given a set of questions for which I had not yet been given the answers. This came as quite a shock to me.

I remember clearly that first week at the university. My tutor gave me a book to read and asked me to criticize it. I wasn't quite sure what he expected me to do, so I asked him to clarify his instructions.

"I want you to read this book," he said, "and then to tell me where you think the author is right and where you think he is wrong."

That seemed strange to me. I wasn't used to this form of education at all.

"But how can I do that?" I asked him. "The author knows far more about the subject than I do—who am I to criticize him?"

Up until that point of my education, I hadn't really learned how to criticize. I knew how to listen carefully, how to learn information, how to organize it in my memory, even how to answer questions that tested my knowledge. But I didn't really know how to criticize.

However, I soon learned. The university taught me how to criticize books, research results, and theoretical papers. And I, quite naturally, transferred that skill outside of my studies. I learned how to criticize politicians, TV programs, church leaders, other students, parents. In fact, I became proficient in criticizing anything and everything that dared to move. I was becoming skilled in the critical method.

The application of the critical method in education is sometimes called "student—centered learning." This assumes that education is a process through which students explore, question, and formulate truth for themselves. When the teacher follows this model of education, she enables the students to work on their own—investigating, discussing, and debating. To facilitate this, the classroom should not contain rows of desks but, rather, different areas where students can work on their own or in groups. In this environment the students are encouraged not simply to accept knowledge from other people but to find it out for themselves, to have their own opinions, to make up their own minds.

The philosopher R. S. Peters argued that education must be distinguished from instruction or training, since the goal is for students to develop a "rational autonomy," the ability to think for themselves and to make their own decisions.[2] That is the aim of the critical method.

The application of the critical method in education is often thought of as a modern development. That isn't strictly true.[3] However, it has only been in the last few decades that this method has been applied in many pockets throughout the educational system.

At the same time, since no part of any culture is an island and all changes in one area tend to affect others, the adoption of the critical method in schools has been mirrored by a shift in other media through which young people are educated, such as TV programs, magazines, youth groups, and churches. In each of these one can see a parallel movement from the didactic model to the critical method.

For instance, increasingly through this period, youth TV programs didn't just expect viewers to sit and watch. They invited them to interact, to respond, to question and criticize. They asked them to express their own opinion. Similarly, teenage magazines increasingly encouraged their readers to question the traditional beliefs and values of mainstream culture.

Even in churches, often condemned for lagging behind the times, the same shift took place. Over the past few decades many churches started house groups where church members met to discuss and debate rather than simply to sit in rows listening to the minister preach. And in church youth groups and Sunday Schools young people were no longer expected to sit and listen but were encouraged to question, to criticize, and to express their own views.

In the last few years there has been pressure to move back toward the didactic model. And the new push to have national standards for what must be learned may also encourage a more traditional teaching style. It is possible that the pendulum may swing completely back in that direction in the years ahead. However, no matter what happens in the future, we cannot change the past.

The fact is that today's teenagers have grown up in an educational world, both inside and outside of school, that is in many cases based upon the critical method. Consequently they tend to be critical. We have taught them how to criticize, and they have become very good at it.

But if that helps explain why they may tend to be critical, it doesn't explain why they can also be cynical.

There is clearly a difference between criticism and cynicism. Criticism is a way of seeking out answers; cynicism is a belief that there are no answers that can be found. Criticism is a methodology; cynicism is a conclusion. Criticism questions other people's beliefs and values; cynicism trashes them.

In the last few pages we have seen one of the major reasons why many teenagers tend to be critical, by looking at some educational theory. Over the next few pages, in order to understand one of the major reasons why teenagers may be cynical, we will have to look at some philosophy.

## A Shift in Philosophy Leads to Cynicism

The idea of philosophy may sound a bit boring. I spend a lot of my time teaching philosophy to older teenagers, and before they get started, most of them assume that it must be about as exciting as tidying their sock drawer. However, they soon realize that philosophy is actually very interesting—because it is about people. It is all about how people think, why they think in a particular way, why they believe what they believe. People don't do philosophy only in universities; they also do philosophy in the bar or on the golf course or over the backyard fence.

So we are going to do some philosophy now. We are going to consider what people think about the big questions in life. To do this, we have to start by looking back in history.

In the Middle Ages (roughly the fifth to the fourteenth centuries) most people simply thought the way they were told to think. Church leaders and others in authority gave people a set of beliefs they had to accept. They were not encouraged or even allowed to question this dogma.

Then things began to change. In bars, over backyard fences, and in universities, people began to think differently. A philosophical revolution took place. The stage was set in the fifteenth and sixteenth centuries, the period now known as the Renaissance, which means "rebirth." But the change really took off in the seventeenth and eighteenth centuries, a time that became known as the Enlightenment or the Age of Reason.

The Enlightenment began with people such as the Italian astronomer Galileo Galilei (1564–1642), who started to use the newly invented telescope and subsequently rejected the dogma that the earth is at the center of the universe. He was ordered to recant and forced to spend the last eight years of his life under house arrest. Subsequently, other writers, artists, and philosophers began to reject other dogmas of the church and placed their hope in the human ability to reason. At this time the German philosopher Immanuel Kant (1724–1804) popularized the catchphrase *"sapere aude,"* which means "dare to be wise." He asked people to risk thinking for themselves. Similarly the French writer Voltaire (1694–1778) called people to be free—to think freely, to act freely.

The Enlightenment ushered in an age of great optimism. People thought we were going to be able to solve all our problems ourselves. As long as we could think freely and act freely, all would be well. The world was going to get better and better. We could find the answers to life ourselves. We could overcome any obstacle. The culture that was based upon these Enlightenment ideals was called "modernism." And this is the world in which we have lived for the past few hundred years.

Modernism placed great faith in the human ability to reason. Rationality was the key idea. Objectivity was sought and prized. So long as we could be set free from the shackles of superstitious church dogma, we would be able to solve our problems through our ability to reason.

For a long time this Enlightenment optimism appeared to be justified. The rationality of modernism saw great advances in science, the arts, and literature. However, in recent years that Enlightenment optimism has faded away. People have begun to realize that the hopes, dreams, and promises of modernism have not been fulfilled. We have not been able to solve all our problems. We don't appear to have all the answers. Consequently, the optimism has turned to pessimism.

Thus Western culture is increasingly rejecting modernism and turning to a new philosophy that is often called "postmodernism." This is not really a proper name for the new philosophy, because no one really knows what it is; we just know that it is "post" (that is, it comes after) modernism.[4]

The term "postmodern" was first used in 1917 by the German philosopher Pannwitz. It was taken up in literary criticism in the 1950s and 1960s, and then in architecture in the 1970s. The most famous formulation of postmodernism was given in Jean—Francois Lyotard's *The Postmodern Condition*, published in 1979. In this book Lyotard defined postmodernism as "an incredulity towards meta—narratives."[5]

According to postmodernism, there are no overall answers. There are not really any answers at all—only questions. Everything is questioned, even the questions themselves. Whereas modernism led to a world viewed as a community of men and women bound together in a common search for answers, postmodernism is leading to a world of individuals floating in a sea of uncertainty.

Jean Baudrillard, the postmodern professor of sociology at Nanterre, says that he sees the world as a party to which an extraordinary number of people have, alas, failed to turn up—and unfortunately these are the people we knew and thought of most highly. Baudrillard writes of what is not there, what went missing, what is no more, what has lost its substance, ground, or foundation. The major trait of our times, he insists, is disappearance. History has stopped. So has progress, if there ever was such a thing. He says the things we live with today are simply the remnants left over. The world, he says, is no longer a scene (a place where the play is staged and directed toward some concrete ending). Instead, it is obscene—a lot of noise and hustle without a plot.[6]

This may sound very academic. One may be tempted to think that postmodernism must be of relevance only to a few isolated (and rather strange) philosophers. However, like it or not, understand it or not, it affects all of us. Our culture has become increasingly postmodern. Let me illustrate this with two examples drawn from everyday culture, one from TV and the other from cinema.

In the world of television there has been a clear move from modern to postmodern programming. Situation comedies have been staples of TV fare for decades. These are modernistic. We see and hear only what the producers of the shows want us to see. There is a definite story line and the show's conflict is resolved by the end of the half hour of the program. MTV, on the other hand, offers a situation show of a different kind: "The Real World."

One of the TV shows most watched by teenagers in the 1990s, "The Real World" is much more postmodern than are situation comedies. There is no script. Instead, cameramen follow around the young adults—a few men and a few women—who are sharing a house by arrangement of MTV. We see them goofing off together, arguing, pursuing their dreams, whatever happens. The show's appeal derives not from a predetermined story but from the unpredictable element that comes from real people interacting.

Similarly in the film world we can see a shift from the modern to the postmodern. Douglas Rushkoff has highlighted this transition by comparing the films *Forrest Gump* and *Pulp Fiction*. *Forrest Gump* is a modernistic film, offering us a sequential, historical journey through the years since World War II. Themes are developed and explored. Messages are communicated. Information is given. *Pulp Fiction*, on the other hand, is postmodern. This film does not tell a sequential story.[7] Scenes take place in the wrong order. Dead characters reappear. We jump from one time to another. As Douglas Rushkoff describes it, "Every scene has elements from almost every decade—a 1950s car, a 1970s telephone, a 1940s style suit, a 1990s retrograde nightclub—forcing the audience to give up its attachment to linear history and accept instead a vision of American culture as a compression of a multitude of eras, and those eras themselves being reducible to iconography as simple as a leather jacket or dance step."[8]

As we can see from these examples, postmodernism leads to chaos. It is born out of pessimism and is maintained by confusion. Therefore, it is deeply unsettling. If we are old enough to have grown up in the years before postmodernism took hold, then we have experienced a security, from modernism, that may help us cope with the postmodern chaos. However, that is not the case for today's teenagers. They are the first generation to have grown up in a world of postmodern confusion. And it has clearly had a massive effect upon them.

"What's the point!" said Andy as we chatted together on the floor of his school's common room. His comment was not a question but a statement. He was not seeking an answer but expressing his pessimistic view of the point-lessness of life. "It's all rubbish; there's no point," he continued. I wish I could say that Andy was an unusual teenager, but his attitude is, unfortunately, typical of many for whom the addition of postmodernism to the critical method has moved them from criticism to cynicism.

Andy was educated to ask questions and to seek knowl-edge by critical inquiry. But, at the same time, he grew up in an increasingly postmodern culture. Through this he had picked up the idea that there are no satisfactory answers that can be given. There is no reliable knowl-edge that can be found. Whether or not he had heard it explicitly stated, he had responded to the clarion call of postmodernism: "We are not seekers after truth—what is the point if there is no truth to find?"[9]

So Andy knew how to ask questions. But he didn't want to listen to any answers, whether they came from me, his parents, or anyone else. And why should we expect him to? He had clearly absorbed the postmodern idea that there are no satisfactory answers, so why bother looking? He knew how to criticize; he knew how to take things apart; but he didn't seem to be interested in putting things together again. His criticism had become cynicism.

Andy had never heard of postmodernism, nor of the critical model of education for that matter. He had precious little insight into why he thought and acted as he did. He didn't really understand it. He just knew that he wanted to criticize things and then cynically declare that they were rubbish.

I never met Andy's parents. But I suspect they were puzzled over Andy's attitude and behavior. Possibly they thought it was their fault. They may have lain awake at night asking themselves, Where did we go wrong? However, if they understood the educational and philo-sophical world in which Andy had grown up, perhaps they would ask a different question: not "Where did we go wrong?" but rather "If these really are the underlying reasons for his attitude and behavior, what can we do about it?"

We will look at a few answers to that question shortly. But before we get there, we need to consider in general terms how we can effectively help teens.

## Helping Today's Teenagers

Luke and Lizzie, my young children, sat on the sled at the top of the steepest, fastest slope in the middle of our snow-covered local park. They pushed off and soon gath-ered speed. I wasn't sure whether they were being brave or foolhardy—because this particular slope had a water-filled ditch at the end of it, and they were not very good at steering. In fact, as the sled picked up speed it became clear that they had very little control over it at all. But they did have an implicit faith in me, whom they had asked to stand in front of the ditch to keep them from falling in.

So there I was with this heavy sled coming straight toward me at high speed. There was no way I would be able to stop it. If I tried, I would get hurt and so would they—and we would probably all end up in the water. So I stood aside. I moved out of the way. And as the sled carrying my children swept past me, I ran alongside them and gently nudged it. That was enough to change its direction. It turned to the left, onto another slope that took it away from the ditch. So they didn't end up in the water. They were safe. I was unharmed. And they were delighted with their extra-long ride.

That is a picture of the task that faces many of us as we try to help today's teenagers. We watch them as they gather speed downhill on a course that will inevitably hurt them and others. If we try to stand in their way, they will collide with us in a huge confrontation. But, if we run alongside and gently nudge them in another direction, we might be able to help them to find another path.

## How to Be Positively Critical

When teenagers are critical, many of us find that we become defensive—or even offensive. Perhaps we want to defend the object of the criticism or to attack the teenager for his attitude. Thus we may respond in a hostile way. For instance, when a teenager looks at something and says, "That's a bunch of garbage" (or other equivalent but more colorful words), we may become defensive and say, "No, it's not; it's perfectly all right!" Or we might go on the offensive and say, "Why do you always have to criticize everything?"

Both of these responses are the verbal equivalent of trying to stand in front of the sled. If we are strong enough, we might be able to stop the teenager—but we are more likely to find ourselves flattened. This may hurt him or us. Either way, it will damage the relationship between us. So, in the same way that it was possible to deflect the sled onto a less harmful route, is there a way in which we could deflect the teenager? Can we stand aside and gently nudge him so that he can find another path? I believe that we can.

If you recall, the problem for teenagers is not so much with the critical method as a methodology (a way of finding answers in the world) but rather with the effect that postmodernism has upon the critical method, in that it tends to lead to a cynical conclusion (a belief that there are no answers to find). Thus the "steep slope" of the critical method becomes a problem because it leads into the "water-filled ditch" of the postmodern conclusion. Perhaps, then, the way forward is to run alongside today's teenagers, helping them to continue questioning along new avenues and new routes—without giving up and coming to cynical conclusions.

When teenagers say, "That's a bunch of garbage," they may appear to be stating a view. It sounds like a cynical conclusion at which they have arrived. But all may not be lost; it may be possible to develop this statement as a way of questioning about the world. If we were to take time to be with them and to gently reply with a question such as "Why do you think it is garbage?" then we may be able to help them to keep on questioning and thinking. More important than that, we will be with them, running alongside them, helping them to question and thus developing our relationship rather than breaking it apart.

This approach means spending more time listening to

teenagers than talking to them. It means making it quite clear that we value their opinions and want to help them think them through and to search for truth. It means joining with them in their search, being alongside them in their questioning.

When I sat on the floor with Andy and made it clear that I really wanted to listen to him, he gradually (very gradually, in fact) began to talk. As he saw that I wasn't going to knock down the things he said but rather was willing to investigate them more fully, he steadily developed the confidence to express himself more clearly. Over time he began to see that it *was* worth searching, thinking, and questioning. Perhaps there *was* a truth to find. When the time came for me to leave, he didn't want to stop. He was no longer in the ditch—he was back on the slope.

Helping Andy was a bit like helping my wife, Carol, buy clothes in a shop. When she comes out of the changing room with a dress on, Carol will have been very careful to make sure that it is all done up properly. It may look as if she is going to wear it as her dress from now on—that is, it may seem that she has come to a conclusion. But really she is just trying it on to see if it fits and she wants me to join with her in asking questions about it. In the same way, often teenagers may seem to have adopted a particular view—they may even state it in dogmatic terms—but they may be simply trying the view on for size, to see if it fits. So they can be encouraged to keep on questioning it, and to build their relationship with us in the process.

This doesn't mean that we don't ever want them to come to conclusions. Of course we do. Eventually Carol needs to choose a dress. It may take a long time (sometimes a very, very long time), but she will have to come to a conclusion eventually. We can't live completely on questions; we can't live totally in doubt. Someone has said that doubt is a bit like the English Channel Tunnel: it is a great way of getting to the other side, but you wouldn't want to live in it.

This is one of the problems that the shift into postmodernism has produced. Postmodernists tell us that there are really no answers to find. Thus today's teenagers are implicitly encouraged to take things apart. But they are not told what to do with the bits; in fact, they are told that there is not really anything they can do with them anyway.

 I believe that we must try to move our culture through postmodernism to a philosophy that is built upon more solid and secure foundations. We cannot stay with postmodernism. It will not last; it is self-defeating. In its very nature it does not claim to be an answer. It is a denial of answers. It is a philosophy that essentially defines itself in terms not of what it is but of what it is not: it is not modern, it is postmodern.

Since postmodernism denies answers and even denies rationality, we cannot just shrug our shoulders and say, "That's the way the world is now." For the sake of future generations, we must return to a search for answers and to a confidence in rationality.

But here lies a major problem. Can we have confidence in rationality? In the days when our culture believed that human beings were created in the image of God we had good reason to have confidence in our rational nature. If God is rational, then so are we: we can trust our brains because God made them. However, if there is no God, if we have simply evolved by chance, there is no reason why our brains should actually be trusted to reason reliably at anything above a basic level.

I am told that Darwin himself recognized this problem. From an evolutionary point of view, one would expect human thinking to be reliable enough to collect food, to mate, to rear young ones, and to control a few other basic activities without which we would not survive. But why should the brain be reliable at any levels of thinking higher than that?

It seems that, for us to be truly confident in rationality, we need to think again about our culture's rejection of God.

We saw that, after the Enlightenment, Western culture assumed that we do not need God—we can find the answers to life's problems on our own. However, this Enlightenment optimism did not bear fruit. We did not find satisfactory and sufficient answers. So we then assumed that there are no answers to find.

But there is another possibility. Perhaps there *are* satisfactory and sufficient answers to life but they can only be found through the Person who created it in the first place.

I am not suggesting, for one moment, that we should go back to premodernism, which was based upon human-centered church dogma. We must not lose the positive insights of the Enlightenment about the value of facts and rationality and truth expressed through testable propositions. Similarly, we must not lose the positive insights of postmodernism about the value of feelings and experience and truth expressed through stories.

Rather, I am suggesting that we should consider whether it is possible to move forward beyond modernism and postmodernism to some kind of holistic culture that recognizes humans as physical, mental, and spiritual beings designed and equipped to live in relationship with the world, with one another, and with God, who created and sustains it all. If God exists, then He will be the source of all facts, the reason for our rationality, the basis of our feelings, the ground of our experience. Perhaps God would also bring His truth to us both in propositions and in stories.

If it were possible to rediscover God in our culture, we would then also find a new model for education— because we would have found a new understanding of the nature of knowledge. The didactic model is based on a dogmatic view of knowledge, as something that the teacher holds and communicates to the pupil. The critical method is based on a relativistic view of knowledge, as something that pupils construct for themselves. However, if we recognized God as the creator and the source of all knowledge, then we would be able to construct a new model for education through which the teacher and the pupil work together to seek the knowledge that is accessible to us in the physical realm (through the sciences), in the mental realm (through the humanities), and in the spiritual realm (through theology).

Such a rediscovery of God may also open up new ways for us to handle the otherwise seemingly insurmountable problem of teenage drug abuse that we face today.

2

# Dancing with Death
## *Understanding Teen Drug Abuse*

*In 1998, 54 percent of high school seniors reported having used an illicit drug of some kind at some point in their life.*
—*Monitoring the Future study[1]*

*"From the pain and sorrow / Of yesterday and tomorrow, / With serenity and peace I hope to find / The once lost piece of my mind."*
—*Matt Shaunfield, dead at twenty-two of a heroin overdose[2]*

Early in the morning of January 12, 1995, Deborah Padgett Barr was awakened by the noise of frantic pounding on her back door. In her bedclothes she raced downstairs and saw her daughter's best friend crying hysterically. The friend said that Deborah's eighteen-year-old daughter, Tish, was in a coma after smoking heroin and crack cocaine.

As she rushed to the hospital, Deborah couldn't believe it. She had suspected that Tish might be smoking pot. But heroin?

As Deborah thought over the past several weeks, however, it began to seem more plausible. There had been warning signs. Although Tish had denied using drugs, she had dropped most of her old friends and had begun hanging around with a new group. The relationship between mother and daughter got rockier and rockier until Tish moved out.

These changes were all the more unaccountable since Tish had always been a good kid and a happy kid. She had a comfortable middle-class lifestyle, earned good grades at school, and had the goal of becoming a psychologist.

Yet as Deborah entered the intensive-care unit and saw her beloved daughter in a coma and hooked up to an array of life-supporting machines, she knew it was true. When she asked why Tish was trembling all over, the nurse replied that it's normal for the body to shake when brain tissue is dying.

A doctor showed Deborah an MRI of her daughter's brain and another of a normal brain. Compared to the normal brain, Deborah's brain was so swollen that it looked as though everything had melted together. Doctors agreed that nothing could be done.

On January 18 Deborah held Tish while life support was discontinued. "With the machines turned off," said Deborah, "I could hear her heartbeat. I held her for a half hour, and then Tish was gone forever."

From other teenagers who had been with Tish when she overdosed, Deborah learned that, although Tish had smoked marijuana before, this was the time first time she had smoked heroin. Once was all it took to bring to an end the life of "a good kid and a happy kid."[3]

There was a time when drug abuse seemed to be mainly restricted to a particular subgroup of young people. Other teenagers referred to them as "druggies" and tended to keep their distance. But this is no longer the case. It is not just those who are rebellious or those from socially disadvantaged families who are using drugs. This activity has become a regular feature of mainstream youth culture. Happily, however, there are some signs that this may be changing.

Reporting on the 1998 national survey results from the Monitoring the Future study of American secondary school students, University of Michigan researchers concluded that illicit drug use by this population is finally heading downward after six years of steady increases. Commented Lloyd D. Johnston, the study's principal investigator, "This turnaround may be due in part to more young people getting to observe adverse consequences of drug use firsthand as the number of users has risen. It may also be due, in part, to more attention being paid to the drug issue by a number of sectors of society, including community groups, parents, government, and the media. One also hears and sees fewer performers in the music industry singing the praises of drugs than was true in the early '90s, which also could make a real difference for teenagers."[4]

Yet while the apparent beginning of a positive trend in

teen drug use is encouraging, the numbers of teen drug users remains high. The same University of Michigan study showed that 29 percent of eighth graders, 45 percent of tenth graders, and 54 percent of twelfth graders admitted to having used an illicit drug at least once in their lifetime. The most commonly used drugs were inhalants and marijuana.[5]

If a teen wants to buy a drug, he normally has little trouble doing so. One survey showed that 45 percent of high school students say they could buy marijuana in an hour or less; only 14 percent said they couldn't buy it at all. Meanwhile, 26 percent of teens say they could buy hard drugs such as acid, cocaine, or heroin within a day.[6] And should they decide to experiment, they will find that the drugs are not only easily obtainable but also easily affordable.

The problems of drug availability and affordability come out in a recent *Esquire* magazine article called "Bad Luck on an Otherwise Fine Night." Writing of a rash of heroin overdoses in Plano, Texas, a suburb of Dallas, journalist Charles Bowden reported, "In the past two years, about a dozen local people, most of them teenagers, have OD'd and died. One local hospital has seen as many as six to eight kids a week who are delivered reeling from enough heroin to put them to sleep forever."[7]

Plano is the kind of community that parents move to in order to protect their children. The crime rate is low. The schools are good. The median income is high. But the lure of drugs is just too strong.

Bowden's investigation showed that for the last decade heroin has been getting both stronger and cheaper. "Right now, heroin on the street is running from 40 percent to 90 percent pure, which means you can afford to snort it and not use a needle." At the same time, there is a global oversupply. "Like the auto industry, the world's heroin labs suffer from overproduction."

In Plano the problem drug is called "chiva," a mixture of high-grade heroin and antihistamine. For openers, you can have it for $2.50 a hit. After you grow to like it, the price bumps up to ten or fifteen bucks. As Bowden comments, ten or fifteen bucks a hit is "no big deal for kids toting their own cell phones and beepers."

And so the young people—in Plano and across the land—go on suffering and dying.

## Dying of Ignorance?

When faced with such dreadful statistics and stories, we know that something must be done—but what? "Education" seems to be the most common answer: we must teach people about the risk of taking drugs. According to this view, if teenagers knew the harm that drugs can do, then they wouldn't take them. This belief is rooted in the ethical philosophy of the Greek thinker Plato,[8] who argued that no one would ever do what is wrong if he or she knew what is right. If we can teach people the right path, then they will follow it—people only do the wrong thing because of ignorance. Thus, the argument goes, if only we can help teenagers to see that taking drugs is dangerous, then they will "just say no."

Consequently, millions of dollars are poured into drug education in the United States. Drug education workers have done a great job in warning people of the dangers of drugs. This must be continued. We are not born with such knowledge; we have to learn that drugs are dangerous at some time—and what better way than through a good drug education worker? But is this the complete answer?

Once teenagers are educated properly, do they stop taking drugs? Do they just say no? Unfortunately not. In my work with sixteen- and seventeen-year-olds, I find that most of them are quite aware of the dangers of drugs. Many of them personally know individuals who are suffering from their abuse of drugs. According to a recent survey, 43 percent of seventeen-year-olds have a friend with a serious drug problem.[9] However, even when they know the dangers, they still take the drugs.

This was clearly illustrated by the case of Helen Cousins. At a New Year's Eve nightclub party in 1996 Helen took a tablet of ecstasy and sank into a coma. She very nearly died. Before she left the hospital, she issued a public warning to all teenagers that drugs were not worth the "dance of death." This was carried in newspapers across the country and she was portrayed as a young person who had learned her lesson and would always, from now on, just say no.

However, only a few months later Helen was arrested for being in possession of amphetamine powder. She and her friends had taken some and then been involved in a car accident.[10] How much more education does she need about the danger of drugs? Is she likely to die of ignorance?

Unfortunately the drug problem will not be solved just by warning teenagers of the dangers. If only the solution were that simple! In fact, if it were that easy, we might have cracked it by now. But we haven't.

We must consider a more difficult route. We must take a step back and look much more deeply at the problem. If

mere ignorance of the dangers is not an explanation, why
is it that teenagers take drugs? What are the root causes
underlying this behavior?

Our first step must be to ask teenagers themselves why
it is that they take drugs. I often do that, and I find that
they usually give me one or more of three different
answers. They tell me that they take drugs to deal with
boredom, to join in with their friends, or to cope with the
pain in their lives.

In a more structured and formal way, researchers at
Columbia University asked seventeen-year-olds the same
question. These teenagers gave a similar response.[11]
Twenty-two percent said that drugs relieve their
boredom,[12] 26 percent said that they took them because
of their friends, and 23 percent said that drugs make them
feel good.

So let's look at each of those three reasons and once
again dig below the surface to see if we can discover
some underlying causes. In this chapter I will look at only
the first two. I will deal with the third reason in the next
chapter, since the underlying cause that we will discover
there leads to other teenage behavior besides drug taking,
and so we will need a whole chapter to think it through.

## Dealing with the Boredom

One might wonder how teenagers could possibly be
bored with their world. The culture in which they live is
far more exciting and stimulating than that experienced
by previous generations. Whereas we grew up with little
streets containing small toy shops, they have grown up
with shopping malls containing massive Toys "R" Us
superstores. Whereas we had a couple of swings and a

slide in the corner of a muddy field, they have huge
theme parks such as Six Flags and Disney World. Whereas
the extent of our sporting opportunities was usually a
swim up and down the municipal pool, they can go to
fully equipped sports centers offering everything from
archery to tae kwon do. Whereas TV offered us few
programs relevant to our age, on small black-and-white
televisions, they can watch nonstop, twenty-four-hour,
high-color youth television on MTV and other cable chan-
nels—not to mention video and satellite.

And yet they are bored! Parents of teenagers know that
one of the phrases they most often hear from their children is "I'm bored." And if parents venture to suggest any
activity to their teenager, this may be dismissed with the
response "Nah, that's boring." Such boredom can lead
teenagers into terribly damaging and self—destructive
behavior.

In 1994 a newspaper ran a story about an eighteen-year-
old boy. On the surface he seemed to have everything
going for him. He was successful in his studies. He had
obtained excellent grades. He was doing well on a new
computer course at college. He also had some good
friends and a loving girlfriend. But he often moaned, "I'm
bored." One night, after drinking several bottles of beer
and complaining that he could "still taste life," he walked
to a nearby railway track and laid his head on the line.
When they found his body, just inches away from it was
his last word, chalked on a stone. It said, "BORED."

Paula was fifteen years old when she was interviewed
by *New Internationalist* magazine. She talked freely about
her heroin addiction and how she now works as a prosti-
tute to fund her habit. When asked why so many young

people take drugs, she replied, "Because there's [nothing] to do. . . . Give us more to occupy us kids so we don't get so bored."[13] We might, quite justifiably, reply, "How much more do you want? How on earth can you be bored when today's world offers you so much that you can do?"

Isn't this the most exciting world that any generation has grown up in? Through the development of computers, for the price of a local phone call we can immediately share images and information with someone in another country. Our stereos can play any music we want to hear, at any time, at any volume. Our TVs can show us events as they happen, anywhere in the world. Meanwhile, scientists are making new discoveries and creating new inventions with dazzling speed. This is the era of nanotechnology and virtual reality. Everything seems to be moving at a breathless pace. And today's teenagers are the first generation to grow up within it. Yet they are bored. Why is this? It is because this fast-paced, nonstop, multimedia world has brought with it a problem—in fact, two problems that compound one another.

First, when people grow up in the middle of this exciting world, they tend to develop an expectation that they must always be excited. They don't expect to be bored. They don't view boredom simply as an inevitable fact of life, something that we can't avoid and must learn to cope with. Rather, they develop the idea that boredom means that something has gone wrong. If they are bored, this is a problem and it must be dealt with. Something must be done to make life exciting again—because life must never be boring.

Second, when people experience a new level of excitement, their excitement threshold tends to increase. However exciting something may be when they first experience it, once they have been there and done that, it tends to lose its excitement value—it may even become boring. So they need something else that is higher or faster or brighter or louder to excite them.

We can see an example of this in the continual development of roller-coaster rides. One is high, so the next one has to be higher. Then one is steep, so the next one has to be even steeper. To start off with, you can ride The Beast at Paramount's Kings Island in Ohio and experience the thrill of a 135-foot drop at a 45-degree angle and a top speed of 65 mph. But if that's not enough for you, you can try out another Ohio coaster, The Magnum at Cedar Point, which has a drop of 201 feet and a top speed of 70 mph. And then, if your hunger for excitement isn't satisfied yet, you simply have to buy your ticket for the Superman ride at Magic Mountain in California. This roller coaster holds the record for its height of 400 feet and its top speed of 106 mph. This coaster is like no other: it goes straight up for four stories and then comes back down backward, giving you the experience of zero gravity for a full six seconds.

Today's TV producers and advertisers have clearly identified this problem. How can they interest people in their program or their product? It has to grip people. It cannot be boring. So it must be more exciting than the last program or the last product. Thus, to beat it, MTV becomes faster and brighter; soaps become more traumatic; films become more violent; and the advertisements tell us that drinking a can of cola is far more exciting than free-fall parachuting or snowboarding or extreme mountain biking. This strategy works, in the short term. But it also continues to push up the excitement threshold. Millions of dollars are spent on programs and advertisements that are ultimately self-defeating. The TV producers and advertising agencies simply keep moving their own goalposts.

Understood in this way, we can see why drugs are so appealing to the generation that has grown up in this fast-paced, multimedia, exciting world. If a teenager has an expectation that she should not be bored, and yet she keeps getting bored, she will find a drug-induced buzz very attractive. If external activities cannot give the rush, why not get it internally? If one cannot feel a buzz indirectly through the things one does or watches or hears, why not get that feeling directly through chemicals? Thus drugs provide the experience of excitement and fulfillment that many teenagers have grown to expect and yet never seem to find. They will give the rush, the pleasure, the thrill. They will banish the boredom.

I have never taken any illicit drugs in my life, and I don't want to. But I have talked to enough drug users to understand how powerfully attractive they are. Some antidrug campaigners try to tell us that, whereas medicine is taken by people who are ill and it makes them feel better, an illicit drug is taken by people who are well and it makes them feel ill. When people say such things, they do not seem to understand what drugs do for the user. Drugs do not make them feel ill; they make them feel good. In fact they make them feel great—for a while. Those of us who have never used drugs look from the outside and see only the shaking, the sweating, the delirium, the risk, the mess, the death. But things look and feel very different for the user.

If you find this difficult to understand, I recommend that you read the novel *Trainspotting*. This best-selling book by Irvine Welsh tells the story of a group of young heroin addicts who will do anything to get their fix. The squalor and degradation is graphically described right from the start. Within the first few pages we find the main character, Mark Renton, in a restroom at the back of a crowded betting shop. The toilet bowl is blocked and the mess has overflowed onto the floor, where others have added to it by standing at the door and urinating into the room. Mark is kneeling in the deep pool of urine, which is soaking up into his clothes. He has his hand down the blocked toilet bowl and he is hunting through other people's half-dissolved feces in order to rescue his opium suppositories, which have just come out with his diarrhea. Eventually he finds them. He wipes them off as best he can. Then, because he is worried about losing them out of his bottom again, he considers eating them instead.[14]

Reading this, and looking from the outside as we do, we may wonder how anyone could possibly live like that. An experience such as this seems so repulsive and revolting that we think it must surely put anyone off using drugs forever. But that is to misunderstand what goes on in the minds of drug users. For them it is not repulsive or revolting. They feel detached from the stench, the mess, the degradation. They feel great.

*Trainspotting* illustrates this by showing us life through the eyes of the drug user himself. Mark describes the effects of heroin by saying, "Take yir best orgasm, multiply the feeling by twenty, and you're still f—ing miles off the pace." Things may look repulsive to us on the outside, but to them on the inside it's a different story.

So it is for teenagers who take drugs to overcome their
boredom. They certainly work. If the teenagers of the
future continue to believe that they must never be bored,
and if their excitement threshold continues to be raised,
then we should not be surprised if they continue to take
drugs.

If we are to deal with the powerful attraction of drugs,
we must tackle this problem of boredom. We will
consider how we might do that at the end of the chapter.
But, before that, we must consider the other major underlying reasons why teenagers take drugs—to join in with
friends and to deal with the pain in their lives.

## Joining In with Their Friends

As we have already discovered and will continue to see
throughout this book, whatever aspect of teenage behavior we seek to understand, it is important that we look
beyond the simple, superficial answers that have often
been given and accepted in the past. In considering what
it means for teenage drug users to "join in with their
friends," we will find that this is no exception.

There is a traditional, simple, and superficial explanation for drug abuse in terms of "peer pressure."
According to this view, teenagers take drugs because
they want to fit in with others around them. Their
friends are taking drugs, so they follow. There is no
doubt that peer pressure is a motivating factor in some
teenage behavior. However, if we think that "joining in
with their friends" is all about peer pressure and peer
pressure alone, we will miss a much deeper and much
more important underlying factor.

When teenagers talk about taking drugs in order to join

in with their friends, most of them do not mean they are blindly following the lead of other people. Rather, they are referring to the fact that they are seeking to be part of a community that together experiences something beyond the limitations of the normal physical world.

Of course, most teenagers will not express it in that way. As with many aspects of teenage behavior, the young people themselves may not have thought through their motives consciously, nor be able to articulate them clearly. However, some have, particularly those who use ecstasy, and it is well worth listening to them.

A teenage girl who is heavily into ecstasy and the dance scene was recently interviewed on TV. She explained why she used drugs and, in particular, described the experience of joining with a group of people who all take ecstasy and then dance together. "The only thing that matters is what's going on at the moment," she said, "and the thing that's going on at the moment is just intense happiness and having a good time. Everybody around you is sharing the same experience—it's very much a collective social thing. You're aware that there are other people across the country doing exactly the same as you, having the same experience. It's good to be part of something that feels that good."

On the same TV program a boy said, "Taking an E makes everyone seem so close, happy, and peaceful. It's like finding a part of yourself you'd forgotten you had. A rave is a spiritual experience; our hearts beat as one."

Ecstasy was once called the "love drug" because of the way in which it removes emotional barriers and inhibitions. It increases the user's awareness, sensitivity, and confidence. This is particularly heightened when it is used in a dance club, where hundreds, perhaps thousands, of young people join together in a collective experience of music, lights, and dance through the night. In this setting ecstasy produces a feeling of togetherness, a sense of community. It induces a collective experience that transcends the normal bounds of this world.

That is why some people describe it as a spiritual community experience. As one put it, "Going to a rave is like going to church. Someone stands [up] front and everyone listens to him. We all need someone to follow. We're just like a congregation—we dance and shout and then afterwards we get together in groups and talk about the experience. We open up our hearts and souls to each other."

Such a spiritual community experience is very attractive to a generation that is looking for a community to which they can belong.

## Searching for Community

Today's teenagers have grown up through the greatest sociological upheaval of all time. In the last few decades the most fundamental fixed points of our society have disintegrated. Whether we look at marriage, the nuclear family, the extended family, schools and universities, or the wider community in general, we find that previously stable structures in the lives of young people have fragmented. Many of today's teenagers, who have lived their formative years during this time of upheaval, are in consequence desperately looking for some kind of community to which they can belong.

Just twenty-five years ago, when I was a teenager, it was considered a terrible scandal if a couple decided that they would live together without getting married. It was called "living in sin" and few people did it. However, since then, things have changed markedly. Increasing numbers of couples decide that they will not marry. In fact, census figures show that in just a decade and a half the number of unmarried couples far more than doubled—rising from 1,589,000 in 1980 to 3,958,000 in 1996. During that same period, the number of married couples rose by only 10 percent.[15]

As marriage has disintegrated over recent years, so has the nuclear family. According to the U.S. Census Bureau, in 1940 just under 5 percent of babies were born to parents who were not married. Fifty years later, in 1990, that figure had risen to approximately 25 percent.[16] Some of these babies are born to cohabiting parents who intend to stay together permanently, but many are not. Furthermore, of those who are born in wedlock, many find that their parents subsequently divorce. Currently, 24 percent of children under the age of eighteen live with their mother only and another 4 percent live with their father only, divorce and marital separation being the leading causes of this single parenthood.[17]

When I was in primary school, everyone in my class had a mommy and a daddy with whom they lived. I had never heard of the word "divorce," let alone understood what it meant. When I moved up to secondary school, one boy in my class told us that his parents had separated. To the rest of us this seemed really strange. We couldn't comprehend it. Twenty years later, when my son went to primary school, he found that many of his classmates lived only with their mommy (and a few lived only with their daddy). Currently, two of his friends are trying to live through their parents' divorce. What will he find when he moves on to secondary school? If present trends continue, he may even be in a minority group—of children who still live with both parents.

There are those who seem to think that we are better off without the nuclear family. They argue that the idea of a mom and dad living together with their children is just a social convention that is now outdated. But that isn't what the teenagers I work with tell me. For them their parents' divorce is devastating. They want to live with both their mom and their dad.

This isn't just socially conditioned; it is biologically conditioned. Each one of them was conceived by a mom and a dad together. They couldn't be conceived by a single mom or a single dad individually, nor by a cohabiting homosexual couple. It took their mom and their dad together to bring them into existence. So they naturally want the two people who conceived them to care for them throughout their growing years. They want to know that their mom and dad will be together bringing them up as they were together conceiving them. If this doesn't happen, they often feel rejected and unwanted.

And yet over the last few decades the nuclear family has disintegrated at an alarming rate. This, in turn, has had a corresponding effect upon the wider, extended family. When parents divorce and one moves out to live in another house, this disrupts not only the relationship that children have with that parent but also the relationships with their grandparents, aunts, uncles, and cousins. Increasingly, grandparents of children from broken families are reporting that they find it hard to maintain contact with those grandchildren who now live with their exdaughter-in-law or ex-son-in-law. The same applies to aunts, uncles, nephews, and nieces.

This breakup of the extended family due to divorce adds to the breakup that is due to the changes in education and employment opportunities in recent years. In past generations the members of an extended family usually all lived in the same town. They would spend much of their lives together. As each child grew up, he or she would go to a local school and then move on to a local job, typically joining relatives to work in the same factory, dockyard, or steelworks.

In recent decades, however, education has increasingly extended beyond the school years to college or university. For many students, this has meant traveling away from home to live in another city. At the same time the demands of the job market have meant that many, of all ages, have found themselves required to move in order to secure employment. Consequently, the members of extended families have been spread all over the country. They may get together again for a short time at special events, but these once tightly knit communities have, over the decades, become increasingly fragmented.

In more recent years another form of fragmentation has taken place in many teenagers' experience of community. This is due to the changes taking place in schools and colleges.

In the middle of the 1980s I began working with older teenagers as a sort of roving chaplain. At that time the schools were vibrant communities in which students would spend their whole day, not just studying but also taking part in a wide range of extracurricular activities, or simply sitting in the common room discussing the big questions of life. In recent years, however, such schools have been restructured. Now many students attend the school only for their lessons, and there may not even be a common room anymore. In the space of a few years many schools have turned from educational communities, where students felt they belonged, into educational supermarkets, where students go for a few hours each day to purchase their educational goods. As they do so, they may talk to the teacher at the counter and a few of the other students in the checkout line, but generally they have little contact with the other shoppers. Here again their community has become fragmented.

If we then look beyond families and schools to the wider aspects of society, we find that these are also increasingly geared to the individual rather than the community. The growth of technology fuels this, as we can now shop by computer, bank by computer, and be entertained by a computer. Internet chat rooms enable computer users to develop "friendships" with people they never meet and whose real names they may never know. It seems as if there is a drive to replace the flesh-and-blood reality of other people with a computer-based virtual reality. As a recent advertisement for a certain hand-held computer game put it, "Not got any friends? Don't worry, with this game you don't need friends."

But we *do* need friends. Whatever technology can do for us, something in us cries out for community. We need somewhere stable where we can belong. This is particularly the case for young people.

Is this not partly the reason for the success of the TV soaps and youth-oriented prime-time dramas? Every day teenagers will stare into their television sets to watch the communities that seem to exist in Capeside, Melrose Place, and Beverly Hills. These appeal to young people who want to be part of a community, to a generation who is desperate for somewhere to belong. And yet they are not real. They cannot be truly satisfying. So teenagers continue to look elsewhere for their experience of community.

The French scholar Michel Maffesoli has written about the growth of what he calls "neotribalism." He says that this occurs where individuals are desperately searching for community and so they group together and sport the symbolic tags of tribal allegiance.[18] For today's teenagers this may be a particular TV soap or a rap group or a designer label. But, as Maffesoli points out, these neotribes are not the stable communities that the ancient tribes were. Membership is easily revocable. The neotribes are transient and always in flux.

Consequently such attempts to create a community always fail to be satisfying. The British sociologist Zygmunt Bauman writes of "imagined communities," which exist only through occasional outbursts of together-ness.[19] Thus one might think of football games, demonstrations, and festivals as imagined communities, where attempts are made to replace the permanent experience of community with temporary community events.

Once again these imagined communities cannot meet our deepest need for a real community to which we belong. Therefore, just as we saw that some teenagers take drugs in order to deal chemically with their boredom, so some teenagers take drugs in order to deal chemically with their search for community. For them, ecstasy promises to deliver the experience of community that they long for. They may not feel that there is anywhere for them to belong in their family, their school, or even elsewhere in society. But when they take ecstasy and join hundreds of others to dance through the night, at last they can feel that they have found a true community of which they can be a member. They have found somewhere to belong.

However, this ecstasy-induced experience is itself only another one of Maffesoli's neotribes, another one of Bauman's imagined communities. These young people haven't really found a true experience of community—just a drug-induced illusion, a chemical con. And when the drug wears off, they are once more on their own—looking for somewhere to belong, feeling the pain of their loneliness.

The desperation of such isolation adds to the other sources of pain that teenagers experience in their lives. They want something to deal with the pain. So they turn again to drugs to try to anesthetize themselves.

## Responding to the Causes of Drug Abuse

To sum up what has just been said, many teenagers take drugs to deal with their sense of boredom and to become part of a community that is experiencing something beyond the mundane material world. How, then, are we to help them?

I believe that we must begin by acknowledging exactly what it is that teenagers have discovered. Despite the constant pressure of this fast-paced, high-tech, multimedia world, they have found that it cannot provide the excitement they seek and expect. So they are looking for other ways to fulfillment. The solution they try is drugs, because these appear to provide what they want. At its heart the problem is not that they are looking for fulfillment but that they are looking for it in a dangerous place. If that is so, then we must help them to look elsewhere.

It would clearly be a mistake to try to push them back into looking for fulfillment in the fast-paced, high-tech, multimedia world. And yet that is what we may be tempted to do. Perhaps we mistakenly think that if teenagers are getting bored with something, then the answer is to make it more exciting. Thus those of us who lead Scout groups or run youth clubs might think that, in order to attract and keep teenagers, we must make our events as fast and loud as the advertisements and MTV. Similarly, parents try to think of exciting places to take their teenagers on vacation. And yet, if we do this, we will then face the same problem faced by the advertisers and TV producers. We will keep moving the goalposts and we will continually need to find an activity even more exciting than last week's, or a vacation destination even more exciting than last year's.

Is it not better, then, to help them keep looking—but to gently nudge them to look elsewhere for fulfillment? But where can we help them to look? Perhaps they already have the answer in the fact that they want to be part of a community that is experiencing something beyond the physical world.

Once again we are driven to the possibility that the answer may be found in the God whom this culture has chosen to reject. If God exists, then might it be possible to find in Him a spiritual fulfillment far better than the dead-end excitement of the modern world or the chemical buzz of heroin? And might it be possible to be part of a spiritual community that is experiencing something beyond this mundane physical world but isn't dependent upon the effects of ecstasy?

Kelly was an older teenager who wanted to be a lighting engineer. In her school she had learned how to run the small, permanent lighting rig in the school's auditorium, and we booked her to run the lights for a Friday night concert by a new band that had been working with me in a series of events at her school. In the middle of that concert I was invited on stage to talk about my experience of God. At the time I didn't realize how intently she was listening in the privacy of the lighting booth. But afterward she came up to me in tears and poured out her heart. She told me how she had for some time been using drink and drugs—and how those substances now seemed to be using her—and she wanted to find another way.

After a long conversation, we prayed together and she cried out to God, not even really sure if He existed, asking Him to show her another way. Some months later she came on one of the residential weekend retreats that I ran for teens in her area. Joining with about a hundred other kids her age, she experienced what it meant to be part of a drug-free community that was seeking spiritual fulfillment in God.

She began to see that fulfillment did not necessarily mean excitement. She began to discover the joy of prayer and the pleasure of peacefulness. She also found that there was an excitement in knowing God and a buzz from worshiping Him with others. But these were an excitement and a buzz that delivered what they promised.

Sometime after this I talked to her and asked her how

her life was going. She told me how, through these
events, she had become a Christian, had joined a church,
and wanted to experience more of God in her life.
However, she also told me that her parents were not at all
happy with this and had done everything they could to
turn her away from God and the church. She recounted
how her dad had said to her, "I preferred it when you
were into drink and drugs rather than all this stuff about
God."

I think her parents had made a big mistake and I urge
others not to do the same. Should we not actively help
teenagers to explore the possibility that the fulfillment in
life they seek may be found in a spiritual rather than a
chemical reality? If that is so, might it also be possible that
God may provide a way for us to deal with the pain in
our lives as well?

3

# "I Feel Like Giving Up"
## *Understanding Teen Suicide*

*"I feel permanently low, I'm not sleeping well and I'm having
problems at school. I can't cope anymore."*
—*from a letter to* MIZZ, *a teenage magazine*

*"One morning you wake up—afraid that you are going to live."*
—Prozac Nation *by Elizabeth Wurtzel*[1]

Kurt Cobain was a happy young child. His mother says
that "he got up every morning with such joy that
another day was to be had." He was well known in the
town where he grew up, particularly for his habit of
marching down the street, banging his toy drum, and
singing "Hey Jude" at the top of his voice.

Everything changed, however, when Kurt was eight years old. His mom and dad separated. "It just completely destroyed his life," said his mom later. He plunged into a depression from which he never seemed able to escape. Even when Nirvana, his band, became hugely successful, he could not be happy. Some days he would lock himself in the recording studio and let out loud screams into the microphone. He developed stomach pains that the doctors were unable to diagnose or resolve. He took illicit drugs in an attempt to dull the physical ache in his body and the emotional pain in his soul. But the pain in his life was so powerful that in the end he bought a gun and killed himself. This is a tragically familiar pattern with too many teenagers.

I had spent a hard day in a school, where I was speaking at a series of events, and had just popped into my office to pick up the mail when the phone rang. "It's Mrs. Cole," said a trembling voice. "I'm sorry to bother you, but it's Lucy; there's something wrong with her and she won't tell me what it is. She is asking for you. Can you come over? She says you'll need to come straight away. Nick, I'm really worried about her."

So was I. I had gotten to know Lucy quite well over the recent months. I was aware of some of the problems with which she was struggling. I knew that her mom and dad had just separated. I knew that she was falling behind with her schoolwork. I knew that she was madly in love with a boy who was now not at all interested in her. I knew something of the turmoil that she was experiencing. Most of all, I knew that she didn't want to live through the pain that she felt right now.

"I'm coming straight away," I told Mrs. Cole and put the

phone down. I ran to my car and drove as fast as I could across town. My mind was racing and my stomach was churning. What had Lucy done? Why wouldn't she tell her mom? Should I have told Mrs. Cole to call an ambulance? Or was I just overreacting?

I pulled up in front of their house, jumped out, and ran up the drive. I tried to appear calm as Mrs. Cole met me at the door and took me in to Lucy, who was clearly very distressed.

"I just don't want to go on anymore," she sobbed. "I've had enough."

I sat down next to her and asked her what she had done.

She took a deep breath and continued, "I've taken a load of tablets."

It was just as I had feared.

That was some years ago. Lucy is now happily married, with her own young family. But she could easily have been yet another statistic on the mounting list of teenage suicides.

According to the U.S. National Center for Health Statistics, in 1994 a total of 1,948 persons aged fifteen to nineteen took their own lives.[2] That represents a quadrupling of the adolescent suicide rate since 1950. And yet the real number of teen suicides is believed by many experts to be much higher than the statistics show since in many states suicides are listed as accidents if there is no suicide note. Many one-person automobile accidents, for example, are believed to in fact be suicides, or "autocides." In any case, suicide is the third leading cause of death for teens, following accidents and homicide.

The figures for teenage suicide have not only been

climbing but also widening. Suicides among younger
teenagers used to be quite rare, but now they are increasing. A study by the Johns Hopkins School of Public
Health revealed that the suicide rate for ten- to fourteen-
year-olds doubled in the years 1980 to 1985.[3]

And these are only the figures for effective suicides. We
must also be aware that many other teenagers make serious attempts at suicide or inflict other forms of harm on
themselves. A study by the National Center for Disease
Control in 1987 revealed that as many as 15 percent of
American teenagers have made a serious attempt at
suicide.[4] The statistics for self-harm are even greater. One
cannot obtain comprehensive figures for the number of
teenagers that deliberately hurt themselves, since many of
them do it in such a way that they don't require hospital
treatment. However, it is estimated that, for every
teenager who commits suicide, about thirty harm themselves in some other way.[5]

As these statistics for suicides, suicide attempts, and
other forms of self-harm increase, we must also take
account of the number of potential suicides that may be
waiting in the wings. In 1991 pollster George Gallup
surveyed high school seniors to uncover their involve-
ment with suicide. The responses indicated that 35
percent had talked or thought about committing suicide,
15 percent had come very close to trying to commit
suicide, and 6 percent had actually tried to commit
suicide.[6]

These are not just statistics in a research report. They
are real people. They may be your child, your niece, your
nephew, or a pupil in your class. I meet them regularly in
my work with teens.

Judy came from a really good home. Her parents loved one another and their children. In fact, they seemed to love all people, even those who were quite unlovely. Uncle Bill was one of those. He wasn't actually Judy's uncle, he was just a neighbor, but Judy's mom and dad had given him that title to make him feel accepted in the family. They also gave him their daughter, Judy, to visit him and take him cakes. They didn't understand why she never seemed eager to go to Bill's house. And she couldn't tell them. She didn't really understand what happened when she was there, but she knew it was something wrong and she thought that it must be her fault.

It was many years before Judy told anyone that Uncle Bill had been sexually abusing her. Judy felt spoiled, unclean, messed up. "It hurt," she said. "It still hurts."

As she grew into her teenage years, Judy started using cannabis in an attempt to deal with the pain. In the years that followed she progressed through a range of drugs, including heroin. But these only numbed the pain for a little while. She began to think about stopping the pain altogether. Over the next few years she made several suicide attempts. "I just don't feel like living anymore," she said. "Nothing could make me feel right again. I just want to get rid of the pain forever."

I have tried to help many teenagers like Judy. We don't have to look far to see why they want to take drugs or even to take their own lives. They want to deal with the pain in their lives, and the source of that pain is very clear. A survey of people who had deliberately taken an overdose found that 67 percent gave the reason that "the situation was so unbearable that I had to do something and didn't know what else to do."[7]

However, there are other teenagers who resort to drugs or suicide without there appearing to be such an obvious reason. Claire was one of these. She spent many of her teenage years stealing Valium from her mother and contemplating her own suicide. In fact, she made several suicide attempts—not really meaning to kill herself at that point but just proving to herself that she could if she wanted to.

Claire knew that there was no one incident that had caused her distress. She hadn't been abused like Judy. Her family had not broken up like Kurt Cobain's. She just felt that she couldn't cope. She didn't feel like going on. The doctors told her that she was suffering from clinical depression.

One might be tempted to think that what we have seen so far in this chapter provides all the explanation we need for one of the reasons behind teenage drug abuse and teenage suicide. Clearly it does provide a good explanation. Some teenagers, like Judy, take drugs or attempt suicide as a way of dealing with the pain in their lives that comes from specific bad experiences. Others, like Claire, take drugs or attempt suicide as a way of dealing with the feeling of pain in their lives that comes from medical problems such as depression.

If this explains it all, then the solutions may seem to be equally apparent. Thus people like Judy are usually offered counseling, and people like Claire are usually offered medication. However, as true as these specific explanations may be, they don't seem to be the whole story. For one thing, they don't account for the rise in drug abuse and teenage suicide. Why is it that the figures should be rising as they are? Is there another factor that has been overlooked? I believe there is. We must look more deeply and consider the possibility that there may be a more fundamental reason for these particular responses to pain.

I would propose that recent medical developments have brought about a new attitude to pain and sickness among many of today's young generation, which means that, instead of enduring pain and sickness and learning to cope with it, they tend to seek a quick solution to it— even if this means resorting to drugs or suicide.

To explore this, we must begin by looking back at some events in history. Once again you may initially wonder what on earth some of this has to do with the problems of teenage drug abuse and suicide. But stick with me.

## An Anesthetic Age

A small group of people had some very strange parties back in the 1840s. For a short time it became fashionable to pass round a pig's bladder containing a special gas for the partygoers to inhale. The chemical name for the gas was nitrous oxide, but it was better known at parties as "laughing gas." It was given that name because of the effect it had upon the person who inhaled it. Once they had breathed it in, they became light-headed and giggly, as if they were drunk. Then they became very sleepy, and if they inhaled enough, they would pass out.

Gradually doctors and dentists began to develop an interest in the effects that this gas could produce. For many centuries they had tried to use drugs of various kinds to reduce the pain and distress of surgery, but none had ever been very successful.

The Greek poet Homer wrote about nepenthe, which

was used in his time. We don't know exactly what this was, but it was possibly a form of cannabis. The Arabian doctors tried using hyoscyamus. This biennial plant, which grows wild on waste ground, contains the crystalline substance known as atropine, which is still used to dilate the pupils for retinal examinations. For many years the surgeons on British ships gave a slug of rum to any unfortunate sailors who had to have their legs or arms amputated.

None of these attempts at pain relief was very good. So the patient simply had to endure the agony while the doctors worked as quickly as they could. There are records of one surgeon working so fast that, as well as amputating his patient's leg (which was his intention), he also took off one of his patient's testicles and two of his assistant's fingers. No matter how fast the surgeon worked, this was clearly a painful process—and the patient simply had to bite the bullet and put up with it.

But in the nineteenth century, nitrous oxide and some other substances seemed to offer the possibility of an effective anesthetic. In 1799, some years before laughing gas became popular at those parties, the twenty-one-year-old chemist Humphrey Davy had inhaled it as an experiment and discovered that it had anesthetic properties. At that time no one had been interested. Some fifty years later, however, doctors and dentists began to try using it in their operations.

In 1845 Horace Wells, an American dentist, attempted a public demonstration of the use of nitrous oxide anesthesia for dental extractions. The demonstration was unsuccessful, but he did cause other medical practitioners to begin experimenting with this gas and with other substances, such as ether and chloroform.

In 1846 William Morton, another dentist, administered ether to a patient having a neck tumor removed at Massachusetts General Hospital in Boston. The success of this anesthetic convinced the medical world that general anesthesia was a practical proposition. Gradually anesthetics became more widely used.

Since those early experimental days, anesthetics have become increasingly sophisticated and gradually more available to all of us in the West. Today it is true to say that we live in an anesthetic age. If we are admitted into a hospital for surgery, we will find a dedicated anesthetist who will give us trichloroethylene or halothane to ensure that we feel no pain. If we go to the dentist for even a small filling, we will be given an injection of novocaine to ensure that the nerves of the tooth are numbed. If we pull a muscle, we will be given ibuprofen. If we have a headache, we can take aspirin or acetaminophen.

Whatever medical problem we face, this anesthetic age tells us, "You should not feel pain." It even seems to tell us, "You should not feel discomfort." The process of fixing the tubes through which the modern surgical anesthetics are delivered is uncomfortable. So the anesthetic age deals with this by giving us an injection of the barbiturate sodium thiopental so that we are relaxed and asleep before the tubes are put in place. Thus even the discomfort of having the pain taken away is itself taken away.

Now don't get me wrong. I love anesthetics. I don't like pain. If I need surgery, I will be thankful that anesthesia has been invented. I am not for one minute suggesting that we should get rid of anesthetics, nor make them less universally available.

What I am saying is that we need to be aware of the underlying effect that this anesthetic age seems to have upon those who are growing up in it—in particular on many of today's teenagers. If we grow up in an anesthetic age, we will tend to develop an implicit expectation that none of us should ever feel pain at all.

When I was thirteen years old, I had to have a lot of fillings put in my teeth. I vividly remember those visits to the dentist. For some of my fillings I was given an injection, but for others I wasn't. I had to learn to put up with a certain amount of pain. If I had lived more than a hundred years ago, I would not have had any anesthetic for anything that was done on my teeth. I would simply have had to endure the pain.

However, today's teenagers have not grown up in the world of a hundred years ago, or even the world that I knew. They have grown up in an anesthetic age. That is all they have known. Consequently, many of them have absorbed the idea that they should not feel pain. If they do experience any, they will tend to seek to have that pain taken away.

## A Sanitized Society

Furthermore, not only is this an anesthetic age, but it is also a sanitized society. The world in which we live tends to give us the idea that we should not experience sickness or death.

In past generations, when people were sick, they were treated at home. No matter how ill they became, they would be kept in the family house. Even when they died, they would die at home. Their children would watch them get weaker. They would even gather around and watch them die.

Today, however, when people are very ill, they are often taken away to a hospital. The children may visit them, but only for a little while. Some parents decide not even to let the children come to the hospital, in case they become distressed by the sights and smells of disease. When the sick person dies, some children may see the death or visit the dead body, but that is increasingly rare.

I know this from some surveys I have conducted. I spend a lot of my time in schools helping teens explore spiritual and moral issues. When we look at the question of suffering, I sometimes ask them whether they have ever watched anyone die—in real life, I mean, not on TV. The result is consistent, wherever I am. Very few of today's teenagers have ever been with someone when he or she has died or have even seen a dead body.

If I had asked the same question a hundred or even fifty years ago, I would no doubt have received a very different answer. Indeed, if I were to ask the same question in many African villages today, the teenagers would look at me as if I were strange. "What a funny question to ask," they would probably say. "Of course we've seen lots of dead bodies."

So, today's teenagers are growing up not only in an anesthetic age but also in a sanitized society, a world in which sickness and death are often hidden from them. Thus many of them unconsciously absorb the idea that they should not expect to feel pain or to experience sickness. If they do, then it is not a normal part of life to be put up with; it is something that has gone wrong and so must be dealt with.

In my work I meet many different people. So I am frequently saying, "Hello. How are you?" I notice that when I do this there is usually a big difference between the answers given by people of different generations. Older people invariably say, "I'm fine, thank you." They reply this way even if they are clearly not fine at all. I recently met the mother of an older teen whom I had been helping. When I asked her how she was, she replied in the usual way, saying, "I'm fine." This was despite the fact that she was in a wheelchair at the time, clearly in considerable pain from a back injury she had just sustained. However, when I asked her daughter the same question, I got a very different answer. She replied, "I feel really rough. I think I've got flu." She clearly hadn't gotten the flu; she just had a sniffle. But to her it seemed like a big illness.

I have lost count of how many students tell me they think they have caught mononucleosis, when really they have just experienced some of the normal aches and pains of life. Many teenagers seem to be very alert to the slightest pain. They seem to expect that they should never feel pain or experience sickness. Isn't this the result of growing up in an anesthetic age and a sanitized society?

## Physical and Emotional Pain

But all teenagers do feel pain. Many of them feel lots of it. And that's because there is more than one type of pain. Physical pain is bad enough, but emotional pain is perhaps even worse. The pain of seeing your parents divorce and your family fall apart is just as great, if not greater, than the pain of surgery or dentistry.

Similarly, they do get sick and die. Sometimes not physically but emotionally. The heartbreak of being rejected feels like a sickness. The experience of abuse makes the victim feel as if some part of her has died.

Paradoxically, in modern society, as physical pain has been taken away, so the sources of emotional pain seem to have increased. As we noted in the last chapter, Western society has become increasingly fragmented. Consequently, greater numbers of teenagers are experiencing the pain of family breakup. As we will see in the next chapter, society has put people under increasing pressure to fit a particular image. So greater numbers of teenagers are experiencing that sickening feeling of inadequacy and rejection. As we will see in chapter 5, modern society's attitude toward sex has increasingly led many into behavior that they later regret and that takes a terrible toll on their lives. So greater numbers of teenagers are experiencing the death of their self-respect.

There is no doubt that teenagers experience a lot of pain today. And it does seem to be pain that is mainly emotional rather than physical. But to the person who is experiencing it, pain is pain. We don't necessarily draw the distinction between physical and emotional pain. So, if we have an implicit belief that we should not feel pain and that any experience of pain must be removed rather than endured, then we will tend to apply that belief to emotional pain in the same way that we do to physical pain.

This seems to be the case with many of today's teenagers. They have grown up through an anesthetic age, in a sanitized society, and so they tend to have a general expectation that they should not feel pain, whether physical or emotional. Their experience of emotional pain and sickness can put them in turmoil. Many of them don't know how to handle it. They just want to get rid of it. Rather than enduring the pain or coping with the sickness, they tend to look for immediate solutions. If they have a headache, they reach for the Tylenol. Are we to be surprised, then, that when they have a heartache they reach for the cannabis or the heroin?

But the source of emotional pain cannot be dealt with so easily. The headache may have gone away when the Tylenol wears off, but the pain of a heartache will still be there when the cannabis or heroin is finished. In fact, when this particular anesthetic wears off, the emotional pain is likely to be even greater. So teenagers may try other ways to deal with their pain. But they find that none of them work. Their pain remains. It even grows. The fact that the emotional pain cannot be taken away itself becomes the source of yet more emotional pain; this can lead to an emotional spiral taking them lower and lower. Nothing seems to get rid of their pain. And nothing will, except death. So suicide begins to look like a good solution. It appears to be the only remedy that will work. It offers the most effective anesthetic. It will deal with the emotional pain forever.

## Dealing with the Pain

When teenagers experience emotional pain, they tend to view it as something that should not be there and so must be removed, by drugs or even suicide. However, it is possible to view pain in another way—as an experience that may bring us to a new understanding of life.

Jess is a young woman who works with me occasionally when I speak at universities. When she was a teenager herself, she was looking forward to a career on the stage as an actress, singer, and dancer. One night she went out to a nightclub with some friends. They had more to drink than they had intended and decided it wasn't safe to drive home. Instead, they went to sleep in the car.

However, in the middle of the night the driver woke up, decided that he was now all right, and thought he would surprise everyone by driving them home while they slept. Unfortunately, he wasn't fit to drive, and he crashed the car. Most of the passengers got away with minor injuries, but Jess was flung out of the door and broke her back.

When she regained consciousness and realized that she was paralyzed, Jess became aware that she had a choice to make. She could cry out to God in anger and hatred, or she could cry out for help. Whichever way she cried, she knew that she would have to wrestle with the question of why this had happened to her, but the "why?" of a seeking hand is very different from the "why?" of a clenched fist.

Jayne works with me regularly as part of my team running youth conferences. Not many years ago, when she was a youth herself, Jayne was engaged to be married to a boy named David. They bought a flat, settled down, and had great plans for their new life together. But then David became ill with a rare heart-lung disorder for which there was no cure. During the months that followed, Jayne watched the health of her young husband steadily deteriorate, nursing him until his death. As she struggled with this terrible experience, Jayne, just like Jess, knew that she could either turn to God or turn away from Him.

Both Jayne and Jess lived with the pain, and still do. Both of them say that, while they didn't want the pain, they know that it has had a transforming effect upon them. Jayne has said on many occasions, "People seem to think that suffering proves that there is no God. All I can say is that my suffering proved to me that God is real—as He came to be with me in it." Similarly, Jess has known a transformation in her life and in the lives of others around her as she has been enabled to live through the pain.

Somehow we have to help other teenagers cope with the pain that they will inevitably face in their lives. We must help them to see it not as an experience from which they must run away but as one they can live through and grow through, as Jess and Jayne both did. How can we do that?

First of all, we must unsanitize society. It is a great mistake to give young people the impression that they can go through life without experiencing pain and sickness—whether physical or emotional. I believe that we should take our children to hospitals. We should help them develop friendships with old, sick, and dying people. We should encourage them to see dead bodies and to mourn with those who mourn. They need to see that sickness and death are not just things that happen on TV and in films, as if they were just some fictional concepts, but rather they are things that we all must face sooner or later.

Second, we must unanesthetize our society. We must learn that pain cannot always be taken away. We cannot run away from it; we have to learn to deal with it.

But most of all, we must help teenagers see that pain and death can be a source of transformation. Every teenager is different and there will be no set way to help them learn this lesson. But in my experience a good way forward is through taking opportunities to let teenagers hear of others who have found pain to be a transforming experience. We can use some of the great stories of history and literature. There are many examples of the transforming power of pain and suffering, from the diary of Anne Frank to C. S. Lewis' lion called Aslan. Or the lesson may be imparted through contemporary real-life stories, such as those of Jess and Jayne—as I have seen many times when they have told their stories to teenagers. Or it can come through the greatest story of the transforming power of suffering—the crucifixion of Jesus.

There was a time when every teenager in our culture knew the biblical story of Jesus' death on the cross. Today, however, many teenagers are unfamiliar with this. And many who know the story fail to see its significance or relevance for their lives.

A good way forward for those of us seeking to help teenagers who feel a sense of hopelessness and despair from the pain in their lives is to help them consider and understand the message of Jesus' death and resurrection—with all that it teaches us about forgiveness, hope, and new life.

If we can help them do this, then we might also be able to help them think again about our own value and that of other people (especially older people), about whom we should want to worship and whom we should strive to follow, about whether we are free to exercise self-control, whether we can be held accountable for our actions, and whether there is any ultimate authority in the world. We will look at these issues in chapters 4, 5, and 6.

4

# Fitting the Image
## *Understanding Teen Vanity*

*In a recent study, 60 percent of sixth-grade girls said they had dieted.*
—*"Images of Women" by Tod Olson*[1]

*"Almost every teenage girl I know is unhappy with her body in one way or another and can tell you down to the minutest detail just what's wrong with it."*
—For Real:The Uncensored Truth about
America's Teenagers *by Jane Pratt*

It was just after nine o'clock when a hundred older teens ambled into their common room. They were going to spend the whole morning with me in one of the youth conferences that I run in schools across the country.

As they came in, many of them were obviously very conscious of one another. Finding the right place to sit was not just a necessity; it was also a fashion statement. They were concerned not so much with how comfortable they would be over the next three hours but with how cool they would look. Some had to sit on the chairs provided, but most would much rather squat on a table, perch on a bench, or recline on the floor so that they could pose and strike just the right image.

Once I had been introduced, I explained that I would like them to join with me in exploring the question of our identity and value. Who are we? What would we like to be? What do we think about our value as individual human beings? And what about the value of others?

I invited them to begin this with a guided reflection. They closed their eyes and I asked them to think about themselves—who they are and what they are like. In particular I asked them to make a mental list of the words they would use to describe themselves. After a few moments I then asked them to imagine that I had a magic wand with which I could change people: if there was anything about themselves that they wanted altered, my magic wand could do it for them. I invited them to make a mental list of the things they would like changed.

I have carried out this exercise with many teenagers, and I find it to be a useful one that helps them begin to gain insight into the way in which they think about themselves. There will always be a wide range of items on their individual mental lists, and I never ask them to share their own thoughts with the group, because this is a personal and private exercise. But through general discussion afterward it usually becomes clear that many of them have used "outside" rather than "inside" words. When they think about themselves, many of them think primarily of their external rather than their internal characteristics.

Many teenagers seem to think of themselves as big or small, fat or thin, pretty or ugly, rather than sensitive or kind or hurt or stable. When they make a list of items they would like to be changed, many of them want to lose weight or have bigger muscles, to have less acne or a smaller nose, rather than be more peaceful, more happy, more reliable, or more loving. This is consistent with the results of recent, more structured research with teenagers.

Joan Jacobs Brumberg, a professor of history at Cornell University, has reported a marked change in young girls' diaries over the past hundred years. A typical entry from 1890 says, "Resolved to work seriously, to be self-restrained in conversations and actions, not to let my thoughts wander, to be dignified, to interest myself more in others." However a typical entry in 1990 says, "I will try to make myself better in any way I can. I will lose weight, get new lenses, good makeup, new clothes and accessories." Dr. Brumberg notes that, whereas in the past young girls thought of "goodness" in terms of character, they now think of it in terms of appearance.[2]

*Psychology Today* magazine in 1997 conducted an extensive survey on body image. This survey revealed that, of young persons between the ages of thirteen and nineteen, 54 percent of young women and 41 percent of young men were dissatisfied with their appearance. For both sexes, excess weight was far and away the biggest area of concern.[3]

"The magnitude of self-hatred among young women is

astonishing," commented the author of the findings, David Garner. "Despite being at a weight that most women envy, they are still plagued by feelings of inadequacy."

Garner continued: "Induction into our culture's weight concerns is happening for women at younger ages. Girls today not only have more weight concerns when they're young, they also lack buffers to protect their psyches. Kids don't know themselves well and have not yet developed many competencies to draw on. It's easier for them to look outside themselves to discover who they are—and find themselves lacking."

Why are so many teenagers so concerned about their external appearance? Once again it is not surprising given the world in which they live. Modern culture is very image-conscious—particularly modern youth culture.

The producers of TV programs and the editors of magazines work hard and spend a lot of money to ensure that their program or their magazine has just the right image. That is how they become popular and attract viewers or readers. They try to catch the mood and style of the moment. They need to ensure that their magazine or TV program fits the contemporary image.

But this is not a one-way street. TV producers and magazine editors not only respond to the mood and style of the moment; they can also have a great influence upon it. They can be part of the process that shapes the contemporary image.

In much the same way, most teenagers work hard and spend a lot of money to ensure that they have just the right image. They too want to be popular; they want to attract friends. However, for them this is a one-way street.

Unlike the TV producers and magazine editors, on an individual basis they are completely unable to influence the mood and style of the moment. A very small number of teenagers may be those rare people whom market researchers call "style leaders." But the vast majority are left simply to fit in with whatever the contemporary image may be.

It is not only teenage girls who are presented with a powerful message about the way they should look. The popularity of young male actors and the success of young male singers provide many boys with an image they feel they ought to match. And here they face a problem. For much of the time, and certainly at the present, the contemporary image is completely unattainable for very many of them. As it is for most people.

According to recent research conducted at Manchester Metropolitan University, most women aged between eighteen and twenty-eight have measurements of at least 35-27-37. However, the average model measures 34-24-34. Similarly, the average woman is five feet, five inches tall, whereas the average model is five feet, nine inches tall. Sarah Beazley, who conducted the study, remarked, "I would say that only around 5 percent of women aged 18 to 28 have statistics similar to those of models."[4]

And yet such models are integral to the image that is presented in Western culture, particularly in teenage culture. For instance, if you look at the front covers of magazines, especially those geared for the teenage market, what do you see? You see models who fit perfectly with the style and image that our culture likes to call "beautiful." When did you last see a magazine with a fat, disabled, or pimply person on the cover?

It is true that for a short period in 1997 fashion magazines did try out a style that was called "heroin chic," with
models who looked as if they were suffering the effects of
prolonged drug abuse. However, although they looked ill,
they also looked "beautiful"—and, in any case, the style
didn't last. Similarly, in June 1997 *Vogue* magazine ran a
photo story with a model who was size sixteen. But she
had clear skin and blond hair and was photographed
from carefully planned angles so that no bulges showed.
Sophie Dahl, the celebrated larger model, does seem to
be in demand, but she is an exception and tends not to
model clothes so much as the "fat issue."

When teenagers look at these magazines, what ideas do
they pick up subconsciously? They cannot fail to absorb
the notion that they, too, must fit this image if they are to
be popular, accepted, and loved. Just as a magazine is
more valuable if it fits the contemporary image, so, the
unconscious logic tells them, they will be more valuable if
they fit with the contemporary image.

Given this state of affairs, it is not surprising that
cosmetic surgery is now such a booming business.
Increasing numbers of people are paying large sums to
have their bodies and faces reshaped by the scalpel or
liposuction tube. Such surgery is not generally available to
the average teenager. But there are other ways in which
they can attempt to change their shape. Is it any wonder
that so many of them develop eating disorders, such as
anorexia nervosa?

This disorder typically stems from an intense fear of
gaining weight, coupled with a distorted perception of
one's own body image. When the anorexic youth looks in
a mirror, she doesn't see the reality of a painfully thin

body that desperately needs more nourishment. Rather, she sees the illusion of a body that is terribly fat and desperately needs to lose more weight. The self-starvation that results can be devastating to the health of the sufferer, and some of them eventually starve themselves to death.

No one knows exactly how many teenagers suffer from such eating disorders. Currently, among fifteen- to eighteen-year-olds, anorexia nervosa is definitely known to afflict about 1 percent of girls and 0.1 percent of boys.[5] However, the real number of sufferers is certain to be much greater than this since one of the major characteristics of the disorder is the desire to keep it secret, which many of them manage to do.

Maureen was very thin when I met her. She had attended a summer festival where I was speaking and she seemed to attach herself to my team for the whole weekend. That enabled us to get to know one another and to talk through some deep issues together. I then met her several more times at various events over the next few years. On every occasion Maureen looked thinner. She soon became painfully emaciated. Eventually, she confessed to me that she had effectively stopped eating. Every evening she told her parents that she had enjoyed a big meal at school and so she didn't want to eat any supper—but in reality she had not had any lunch either. In common with many who suffer from eating disorders, she wanted to keep it to herself, and it was a big step forward for her to tell anyone about it. Thus began her long, slow process of recovery.

Eventually Maureen began to see herself as she really was, not in comparison to some impossible image which she tried to fit. The key for her was to begin to see herself in a new light—to look at herself differently. I helped her to recognize another image for herself, an image that was not about her external appearance but about her internal qualities.

The image that I helped Maureen to consider is an image that has been largely rejected by Western culture in recent years.

## Whose Image?

Psychologists tell us that there is no doubt that human beings have a powerful desire to worship someone or something outside of themselves. Whether it is the hero worship of a fourteen-year-old boy for the eighteen-year-old captain of the girls' volleyball team, or the adoration of that seventeen-year-old for the lead singer of her favorite band, there seems to be an inherent desire within us all to worship and adore someone or something.

This internal drive may be linked to the fact that people are instinctively religious. Wherever one travels in the world, people seem to have a built-in desire for God. Throughout history people have sought to find a spiritual reality beyond themselves. Looking back on his own spiritual search, Augustine described it in this way: "I carried with me only a loving memory and a desire for that of which I had the aroma but which I had not yet the capacity to eat."[6]

If we still lived in a culture that encouraged us to seek for God, we might find our spiritual fulfillment in a spiritual realm. But what happens if we grow up in a culture that has rejected God? We still want something or someone to worship. We still seek images and icons to focus upon. But where will we find them? Clearly not in heaven. So it has to be here on earth. Thus we look for people whom we can worship and adore—people whom we can strive to follow. Today's teenagers have grown up in just such a world—a world in which God has been rejected and replaced with other objects of worship.

On August 31, 1997, the world was shaken with the tragic news that Diana, Princess of Wales, had been killed in a car crash in Paris. Throughout the following week London became the focus for pilgrims traveling from all over the country to bring flowers, cards, and tributes. Melvyn Bragg observed that many of the inscriptions on the cards referred to Diana with "adoration as to an idol." Indeed, many not only echoed the statement expressed on the day of her death that "a light had gone out in the world," but also extended it to say that "she was the light of the world."[7] The messianic overtones were unmistakable. On the day after Diana's funeral, the journalist Melanie Phillips commented that the events of the week had "shown a profound spiritual emptiness which people want to have filled."

Indeed emptiness always will be filled, in one way or another. Thus the reaction to Diana's tragic life and death was one example of the way in which our culture seeks and provides icons and images that we can worship and follow. Teenagers will gaze lovingly at the posters of their favorite band. Successful athletes and actors are interviewed on TV and asked for their views on moral, social, or political dilemmas—not because we really think that the ability to run fast or act well qualifies them to answer these difficult questions but because somehow we have a desire to follow them and to be like them.

Thus those we worship and follow provide for us a sense of identity, purpose, and meaning. They give us an image of how we would like to be and how we think we ought to be. The images that are provided by these contemporary objects of our worship are very different from those derived from the objects of worship in past centuries.

For many years Western culture was built upon its Christian roots and the set of beliefs that stemmed from them. The Christian tradition taught us that God was our Creator; it was Him we should worship and it was from Him that we would derive our sense of purpose, meaning, and fulfillment. The explicitly clear Christian teaching about our identity told us that our image came from God, since we are all "created in God's image."

There was a lot of theological debate about what exactly it meant to be made in God's image, but it was always clear that this referred to our internal nature and not our external appearance. People did not believe that we look like God but that we were created with God's nature in some sense stamped upon us. They believed that humans have many of God's characteristics, such as the capacity to love and be loved, to think, to feel, and to act freely. These internal characteristics were considered to be fundamental to our humanity. Thus our internal character was reckoned to be much more important than any external appearances.

However, in recent years this Christian heritage has been largely rejected. We now live in a post-Christian culture. This has had many different consequences, as we discover in later chapters of this book. But one consequence that we need to consider here concerns our belief about who we are. If the Christian belief that we are created in the image of God has been rejected, in whose image should we be? Who are we as human beings? What is our value and worth? What is our identity and meaning?

For most people the focus of our identity and meaning, our value and worth, has shifted from our internal nature to our external characteristics. As someone said recently, "If we were created in God's image, why does everyone want to look like Cindy Crawford?" The fact is that our culture now does not believe that we were created in God's image, so it has replaced an internal model from God with an external model from the catwalk.

This rejection of the Christian worldview has sometimes been called "the death of God." The stage was set for it by the Enlightenment of the seventeenth and eighteenth centuries (see chapter 1). Through the Enlightenment, Western culture rejected the dogma of the church. A century later Western culture rejected God Himself.

The main character behind this was a German philosopher by the name of Friedrich Nietzsche. Nietzsche was born in 1844, the son of a Lutheran pastor. When he was twenty, he went to the University of Bonn to study theology. But Nietzsche was not to become a theologian, nor a pastor like his father. In fact, he became quite the opposite, writing books such as *The Antichrist* and *Beyond Good and Evil*. In these and his other writings he rejected Christian belief as the product of a people who think like slaves—weak people who encourage gentleness and kindness because this serves their interests. He called people to think instead like masters who are strong and independent.

In his book *The Joyful Wisdom*, published in 1882, he

expressed this belief in the phrase for which he is most well known. "God is dead," he wrote. "The belief in the Christian God has become unworthy of belief." A few years after this, Nietzsche collapsed in the streets of Turin, having lost control of his mental faculties completely. He spent the last eleven years of his life deranged, first in a Basel asylum and then in the care of his mother and sister. He died in 1900 from a paralysis probably caused by dormant tertiary syphilis.

Nietzsche ended his years as a sad, sick old man. But his ideas have lived on. They have had a profound effect upon Western culture. The *Encyclopedia Britannica* describes him as "certainly one of the most influential philosophers who ever lived." His views have been a major driving force behind the march of atheism and the rejection of the foundations of Christian belief in the Western world.

A recent poll revealed that, while nearly all teens believe in God (95 percent), only about three-quarters (76 percent) conceive of Him as a personal God. In addition, less than a third of teens (29 percent) claim to have personally experienced the presence of God.[8] About two-thirds of teens believe that it doesn't matter what religious faith you follow because all faiths teach similar lessons.[9] The fact is, in our post-Christian culture most people have rejected historical Christian beliefs. One of those is the belief that we are created in God's image.

It has been over a hundred years since Nietzsche first wrote about the death of God. But it is only recently that such a view has become widely accepted. Nietzsche himself recognized that this would take a long time. To him it seemed as if God was dead but He wouldn't lie down. Nietzsche gave the name "passive nihilism" to the fact that people did not yet realize that religious absolutes had dissolved. He said that people are bound to be reluctant to accept the death of God because to do so also means accepting that their lives are essentially purposeless and meaningless.

But here we are, some hundred years later, in a culture that does seem to have accepted Nietzsche's beliefs. Teenagers are therefore growing up in a culture through which they learn that their lives are fundamentally purposeless and meaningless—as we see when we look at the beliefs of many contemporary scientists and philosophers.

## So, Who Are We?

Some try to tell us that we are simply animals. They argue that we may have evolved to a higher degree of sophistication than the other animals, but other than that there is nothing very different or special about us—we are just another form of animal. Desmond Morris, the famous zoologist, put it this way: "There are one hundred and ninety-three living species of monkeys and apes. One hundred and ninety-two of them are covered with hair. The exception is a naked ape self-named Homo sapiens."[10]

There are others who try to tell us that we are simply a set of chemicals and neurons. Francis Crick proposes what he calls the "astonishing hypothesis" that "you . . . your sense of personal identity and free-will, are in fact no more than the behavior of a vast assembly of nerve cells and their associated molecules."[11]

There is no doubt that our brains do contain chemicals and neurons. And these chemicals and neurons do code and carry information. Some like to use Richard Dawkins' term "memes" for such units of information.[12] But Francis Crick and others are trying to tell us that this is all that there is. There is nothing more. There is not even a real "me" who truly exists. Susan Blackmore, a psychologist based at the University of the West of England, has said, "The idea that we exist is an illusion"[13] and "The answer to the question 'Who am I?' is simply 'I am one of the many co-adapted meme-complexes living within this brain.' "[14]

Finally, others try to tell us that we are simply evolutionary byproducts. Sir Fred Hoyle, the astronomer and mathematician, put it this way: "[We are] no more than ingenious machines that have evolved as strange byproducts in an odd corner of the Universe." Richard Dawkins, the evolutionist, declares that we are "machines built by DNA whose purpose is to make more copies of the same DNA. . . . [This] is every living object's sole reason for living." According to him, the human body is created by its DNA merely so that the DNA can reproduce itself—we are a massive, but necessary digression.[15]

When launching his book *Climbing Mount Improbable*, Richard Dawkins said in a lecture, "It seems like a pointless point, and it is. . . . There is no fundamental purpose in life."[16] At the end of his book he tells of an occasion when he was driving through the countryside with his six-year-old daughter. They looked at the wildflowers and Dawkins asked her what she thought they were here for. She told her daddy that she thought they were here to make the world pretty and to help the bees to make honey for us. Dawkins says, "I was touched by this and sorry that I had to tell her it wasn't true." He thinks it isn't true because he believes that the only reason anything is here is so that it can pass on its DNA. It seems like a pointless point and it is.

He was sorry to tell her this. We can only imagine what his daughter felt to hear it. But I do know what teenagers feel when they think about such ideas, because they tell me quite frequently. There are some who say that they wholeheartedly embrace one of these views. Such as Amanda, a very bright student who told me that she was a great fan of Richard Dawkins. She proudly announced her belief that we are simply biological mechanisms whose only purpose is to pass on our DNA. I tried to help her to think through what that meant for her significance and value—and the significance and value of other people in her life. I asked her how she expects to react when her mother dies; will it mean nothing because her mother was only a biological mechanism that had already passed on its DNA? She said, "I will probably cry, but that itself is only a biological reaction—it means nothing." At least that's what Amanda said with her lips. Her eyes were telling a different story. Clearly, her heart was troubled.

So we face a crisis in our culture. Who are we? What is our value and significance? Whom should we worship and follow? We have rejected the historic Christian belief that we should worship God and try to develop God's characteristics in our lives. We have rejected the view that we are created by God in His image, with all the significance and value that this entails.

This is the world in which today's teenagers have grown up. It is the only world they have known. Those of us who are older grew up in a culture that still held on to its Judeo-Christian heritage. We were taught about (even

instructed in) Christian faith at school, and most of us
went to church occasionally, if not regularly. We may
have rejected Christian faith as we grew up, but the foundations were still there in our lives. Deep down we probably had, and still have, the inner sense that we are made
in the image of God and that our internal character is
more important than our external image.

But this is not generally so for today's teenagers. So
many of them seek after and idolize other gods; they find
other icons to adore—Princess Diana or Michael Jordan.
And they find other images in which they wish we were
made—Kate Moss or Brad Pitt. It is inevitable, though,
that this will lead to problems in their lives, for these gods
are inadequate and unfulfilling.

The current icons of teenage culture are distant.
Whereas the Christian understanding of God showed Him
to be available for us so that we can come to know Him
and experience Him personally, these icons are locked
away in palaces and mansions, surrounded by body-
guards who will keep the worshipers at a safe distance.

Similarly, the current images of teenage culture are unattainable. Whereas the Christian understanding that we are
created in God's image brought with it the knowledge
that our internal characters can become like His, the
external image of the supermodel will always be beyond
the reach of almost all of us.

Finally, these objects of worship are obviously faulty.
Whereas the Christian understanding of God showed Him
to be pure and perfect, we all know of sports stars and
pop stars who have fallen off their pedestals.

Many of today's teenagers are left with a vacuum. A
vacuum filled with image rather than substance, with its

focus on external appearance rather than internal character. And this inadequate filling takes its toll in their lives. It
has a profound effect upon the way in which they view
and treat their own bodies.

## Presenting the Possibility of God

For centuries people in the West worshiped God and
aspired to follow Him, thus seeking to change their character and inner nature. In recent years, however, as God
has been rejected, people have worshiped pop stars,
athletes, and supermodels—and have aspired to follow
them, thus seeking to change their image and external
nature.

So, faced with that problem, how can we help today's
teenagers value internal character rather than external
appearance? We might think that the answer lies in education: perhaps we should ask the schools to teach about
the value of internal character rather than scholastic
attainment. Or we might think that the answer lies in the
home: perhaps we should teach parents how to reward
and develop good character rather than good skills, gifts,
and abilities. Or we might think the answer lies with the
media: perhaps we should encourage films and TV
programs that celebrate internal character rather than
external appearance. Or we might think the answer lies in
the fashion industry: perhaps we should encourage the
modeling of good character instead of good figures.

All of these practical approaches may be valuable for
today's teenagers. However, each of these explicit
attempts to teach the value of internal character will find
itself struggling uphill against the powerful implicit
message that internal character is not so important. This

message derives from the fact that the culture tells us the nihilistic message that we are accidentally evolved bundles of chemicals and neurons with no ultimate value other than that which we choose to ascribe to ourselves. We must deal with this.

And the way to deal with this, ultimately, is to work at changing the perception that God does not exist, or that if He does, we can live as if He does not. Teenagers are usually open to hearing about the spiritual experiences of others. We can take advantage of that openness to tell them how we have found that God is real and that He gives our lives meaning. We can explain how a relationship with God through His Son has helped us look at ourselves in a different way and change our image of who we should be trying to become.

It's not that we should not try to help teens understand scriptural teaching on God; it's just that a personal witness to God is often the most effective starting place with today's young people. And you might be surprised at how effective it is.

The news that we're not mere biological mechanisms should come as a great relief to people who have bought into that severely limited idea of human nature. We are creatures of dignity, made in the image of God with a soul as well as a body. While physical beauty is a fine thing, people are on firmer ground if they focus on fitting the image of Jesus spiritually than on fitting the image of whatever celebrity represents our physical ideal. Physical beauty is a temporary state for even the most stunning supermodel. Spiritual beauty is within reach of anyone who commits to God, and it lasts forever.

The news that life need not be purposeless and meaningless should likewise come as a relief. God made human beings with a drive to accomplish things, and if we can awaken hope in teenagers that life can be meaningful through God, the dissatisfaction with one's outward appearance should begin to pale in significance. Teens are at a time in their lives when they are looking forward to what they are going to make of their lives. A restored sense of purpose is just what they need and want as they face the future.

While the nihilism of today's teenagers can be terribly difficult to overcome, it's not impossible. It's a little like a Christian missionary preaching about Jesus to a people who have never heard of Him and who have a belief system very different from the one presented in the Bible. The labor is hard and slow at first, and the missionary may entertain thoughts of giving up, but in fact he is not working alone. God's Spirit is simultaneously working in the hearts of the people to draw them toward God. And thus, one by one, some people finally understand what the missionary has been saying to them, want the Lord he has revealed to them, and put their faith in Him.

If we can work at changing teenagers' fundamental nihilism—their outright or practical disbelief in God—they may finally have a basis for believing that they have a value apart from their physical appearance. They may begin trying to conform to the image of Jesus rather than that of the pop star whom they currently most admire. They may become beautiful in their own eyes and the eyes of God.

As we will see in the next chapter, a renewed focus on internal and spiritual realities is also needed to help teenagers change what they do with their bodies.

5

# Just Do It
## *Understanding Teen Sex*

*Just over 13 percent of all U.S. births are to teens,*
*and of these births, 76 percent occur outside of marriage.*
*—The Alan Guttmacher Institute[1]*

*In 1992, 295,000 teenage women (ages fifteen to nineteen)*
*received abortions. This figure means that around one-third of*
*all pregnancies in this age-group ended in abortion.*
*—Statistical Abstract of the United States[2]*

"Shut up talking about love—there's no such thing."
This aggressive outburst in one of my youth conferences was quite unexpected. At the time I was discussing with the teenagers the teaching of Jesus, one of whose

greatest commandments was that we should love one another. One girl obviously couldn't accept this and so she shouted, "How can love be so important when it doesn't exist?" I invited her to say more, but her eyes then filled with tears and it was clear that she didn't want to.

Later that afternoon the head of the school whispered in my ear some reasons why this girl had such an attitude toward love. She had recently been dumped by her boyfriend—as soon as he discovered that she was pregnant. She had subsequently had an abortion and was now suffering from some of the symptoms of what is known as "postabortion trauma." Her hopes and dreams of love had been shattered. Over the space of a few weeks she had changed from a happy, vibrant girl who was enjoying life to a depressed, cynical girl who no longer believed in the existence of love.

She is one of thousands of teenagers whom I have tried to help overcome the tragedies that their sexual activity has brought into their lives. Some have had abortions, some have had babies, some have picked up sexually transmitted diseases. Many others have avoided all of these obvious dangers but have found themselves incapable of escaping the unexpected psychological, emotional, and spiritual consequences of their sexual activity.

Tina was a virgin when she arrived at her older teen years. She was quite certain that she had worked out her attitude toward sex. She had talked it through with her mother and had decided that she would not sleep with any boyfriend unless they had been going out together for six months and she was completely sure that they were in love with each other.

On her first day in school, one year, she noticed a boy and took a liking to him. They soon started going out together. The relationship developed and she felt sure that they were in love with each other. After six months, they slept together. However, in the weeks that followed, their relationship cooled and they broke up.

Soon afterward Tina started going out with another boy. The relationship developed and, after just two months, she slept with him. She knew they weren't in love and she knew that she was going back on her decision to wait for six months, but somehow she just couldn't stop herself. Once more the relationship ended. And she started going out with someone else, whom she slept with after just two weeks. The saga continued and she soon found herself going out with a series of different boys and sleeping with them all. It wasn't unusual for her to meet someone at a party and then go straight home to bed with him.

Tina told me that, throughout all this, she hated herself for what she was doing. Each night she would lie in bed thinking, What a tart I have become. But she just didn't seem to be able to stop herself. She didn't have a baby; she managed to avoid all the sexually transmitted diseases; she didn't get AIDS. But psychologically, emotionally, and spiritually, she knew that she was steadily destroying herself.

Tina felt that her heart had been broken through her sexual activity. There are many teenagers like her. But there are many others who are not. They will tell me that they sleep around with lots of different partners and yet they are not brokenhearted. They don't lie in bed at night hating themselves for what they are doing, as Tina did.

They say that they are not falling apart because of their sexual promiscuity. Why is this? I find, as I talk more fully with them, that they are clearly telling the truth. But they are only telling part of the truth. They have not become brokenhearted, but they have become hard-hearted.

Trevor was sexually promiscuous and proud of it. He was one of the first of the group of guys he hung out with who managed to go the whole way and sleep with a girl. He wasn't really going out with her; he didn't really care about her; he just wanted to know what it felt like to have sex with a girl. And it felt good. Over the next few years he slept with lots of different girls. With some of them he actually went out with them for some time and began to form a real relationship with them. But it never seemed to last. He soon felt driven to make another sexual conquest.

Trevor recalled later that, during this time of sexual promiscuity, he seemed to spend as much of his time trying to get rid of a girl that he had slept with as he did trying to find another. In fact, he often didn't even enjoy the sex because, while he was doing it, all he could think about was how he was going to dump the girl afterward. When he stopped and reflected on his sexual activity, he realized that he didn't really enjoy any of it much anyway. Sure, there was the fun of the chase and there was the thrill of the orgasm. But somehow it all seemed so empty, so hollow, so unfulfilling.

Trevor didn't feel brokenhearted like Tina did, but when he allowed himself to think about it, he realized that he did feel hard-hearted. He knew that his sexual promiscuity was taking a toll in his life. He was becoming harder and more lonely in his heart. He never seemed able to become attached to a sexual partner. And he wasn't sure that he ever would be. He seemed to be squeezing out any feelings he had, other than that feeling of cold, raw sex. As he lay in bed at night he didn't feel broken. He didn't feel anything much at all. But he wanted to. He wanted to be warm again. He wanted to be vulnerable, to be intimate, to be romantic, to be passionate.

Both Trevor and Tina were clearly damaged by their sexual activity. The effects were not physical; they were psychological, emotional, and spiritual. But they were real. And they are all too common.

Research organizations looking into teen sexual behavior describe a youth population that is more sexually active than many adults would suspect. They report that most young people begin having sex in their mid to late teens. Indeed, by twelfth grade, about three-quarters of all boys (77 percent) and about two-thirds of all girls (66 percent) are sexually active.[3] A quarter of all teens aged fifteen to nineteen reported having sex several times a week on average. Another 19 percent reported having sex once a week on average.[4] It is no wonder that every year 3 million teens—about one in four sexually experienced teens—acquire a sexually transmitted disease.[5]

Nor is it any wonder that teenage pregnancy is commonplace. In fact, teen pregnancy rates are much higher in the United States than in many other developed countries—twice as high as in England or Canada, and nine times as high as in the Netherlands or Japan. Each year almost 1 million teenage women—11 percent of all women aged fifteen to nineteen and 20 percent of those who have had sexual intercourse—become pregnant.[6]

As for the outcomes of all these pregnancies, the Alan Guttmacher Institute reported the following figures for

1995: among pregnant women between the ages of fifteen and nineteen, 263,750 of their pregnancies ended in abortion, 126,360 ended in miscarriage, and 499,873 ended in live birth. These figures are actually an improvement over similar statistics from twenty years previously. In 1975 there were higher numbers in all categories (326,780 abortions, 149,130 miscarriages, and 582,238 live births).[7] But of course the figures on pregnancy outcomes, like the figures on teen sexual activity in general, remain disturbingly high.

So, why do they do it? Why are so many teenagers sexually promiscuous? There are many reasons. We don't have to look far to see some obvious causes right there on the surface of teenage culture.

The first obvious reason is biological. It has to do with the teenagers' hormones. In the preteen years most boys, for instance, are not sexually alert. They view their penis simply as a pipe through which they urinate and they fail to comprehend what pleasure could possibly be derived from the things they learn about in their sex education lessons at school.

But then something happens. Hormones start to flood through their bodies and their sex drive seems to switch on at full power. Suddenly they can't even ride on a bus without having a throbbing erection. They become acutely aware of the pleasurable feelings that their penis can give. Their nights are suddenly full of sexually explicit dreams, and they experience their first nocturnal emissions.

What has happened to them? The answer is biological. Their body is now full of hormones. And they feel a physical drive toward expressing and experiencing their sexuality.

The second obvious reason is psychological. It has to do with the teenagers' curiosity.

To young people the world appears a bit like Disneyland. It is full of different opportunities and experiences for them to try. When they are young, they enjoy the rides in "play world." Dolls, trains, toy cars, and coloring books fill their minds. But then, as they grow into their adolescence, for the first time they notice the signs to "sex world." When they look into this land, they see before them huge new rides that they never knew existed. They are full of curiosity. They want to try them out. They want to know what they feel like.

The third obvious reason is sociological. It has to do with their desire to be accepted by those around them.

There is no doubt that teenagers are desperate to fit in. They want to be accepted within their peer group. They cannot bear the idea of being stigmatized for being odd or different in any way. So, if others are boasting of their sexual experiences, they will not want to be left out. It has been said that we live in a culture in which "no sexual activity is considered deviant—except no sexual activity." That is, it is acceptable to engage in almost any kind of sex, but if you are not sexually active somehow, there must be something wrong with you. For some teenagers, therefore, virginity is a stigma to be lost as soon as possible. So, for them, the reason for their sexual behavior is sociological—they want to fit in.

All three of these reasons are dealt with in detail in many other excellent books about teenagers. If you want to read more about them, there are plenty to choose from. I would recommend *Sex Matters* by Steve Chalke (Hodder & Stoughton, 1996). However, as important as these three well-known reasons are, there are other explanations for sexual promiscuity. In particular, there is a more fundamental, philosophical reason why many teenagers, especially, are increasingly promiscuous. This reason does not seem to be covered in books about teenage sexual behavior. Perhaps it has not yet been recognized or understood by most people. This should give us cause for concern, because this reason is potentially much more damaging to teenagers and our society in general than are any of the other more commonly stated explanations, for it has implications for all sorts of potentially damaging behavior, not just in the area of sexual promiscuity.

To understand this reason we must, once again, take a step back and think about some of the underlying beliefs that have developed over the centuries but that have only really made it into popular culture in recent years. As we consider these, over the next few pages, we will need to look at some science and some philosophy. Once more, you may wonder what this has to do with teenage sexual behavior. But stick with it and all will become clear.

## Science and Sex

During the last few centuries, people have developed a high regard for science. Today it seems to provide us with so much. We drive in cars and fly in planes. If we get sick, we take antibiotics or have laser surgery or install pacemakers. It is tempting for us to think, then, that science will give us all the answers to life.

Although science is actually only a methodology (a way of asking a particular small set of questions about life), there has been a strong tendency in Western culture to accept it as a philosophy (a belief that these questions are the only ones worth asking). This philosophy is variously described as "scientism" or "scientific materialism" or "naturalism." For our purposes, let's concentrate on the notion of naturalism and see where this particular philosophy is leading our culture and the teenagers who are growing up within it.

Naturalism is a belief (a statement of faith) that what we can study by means of the natural sciences is really all there is. According to naturalism, there is no need to look beyond or outside the physical world for any supernatural explanations. This rules out any belief in God or a spiritual reality. It even seems to reject the traditional view of a human soul that in some way transcends the limits of the physical world.

Nicholas Humphrey, the distinguished theoretical psychologist, put it this way: "Few adults in the modern world can actually be unaware that there are now physicalist explanations for most if not all natural phenomena, not excluding the workings of the human mind."[8] Friedrich Nietzsche expressed it in more emotive terms: "I am body and soul—so speaks the child. . . . But the awakened, the enlightened man says: I am body entirely, and nothing beside; and soul is only a word for something in the body."[9]

Naturalism has therefore been presented to our culture as a grown-up response to life that will take us beyond the silly superstitions of the past. It is seen as the logical conclusion of the wonderful science that has brought us so much, and will continue to in the future—if only we will trust it.

Carl Sagan described science as a candle in the darkness

that can "routinely predict a solar eclipse, to the minute, a millennium in advance. You can go to the witch doctor to lift the spell that causes your pernicious anaemia, or you can take Vitamin B12. If you want to save your child from polio, you can pray or you can inoculate. If you're interested in the sex of your unborn child, you can consult plumb-bob danglers all you want . . . but they'll be right, on average, only one time in two. If you want real accuracy . . . try amniocentesis and sonograms. Try science."[10]

The missionary zeal of Carl Sagan and others has clearly had an effect upon contemporary culture and those growing up within it. Pollster George Barna discovered that, among teens who don't identify themselves as born-again Christians, 83 percent believe that people can earn a place in heaven by being good. Furthermore, two-thirds believe that Satan is a symbol of evil and not a living being.[11] Barna's fellow pollster George Gallup adds the observation that only about two-thirds of all teens (67 percent) believe in life after death.[12] Less than half go to church (41 percent attend Sunday School and 36 percent attend a church youth group).[13]

Despite the phenomenal success of "The X-Files," it would appear that most teenagers would identify with the natural explanations of Dana Scully rather than the supernatural ones of Fox Mulder. It seems that most of today's teenagers have adopted this fundamental underlying belief in naturalism.

What difference will that make to their sexual behavior? Before we can begin to consider this, we need to understand two characteristics of beliefs in general.

First, individual beliefs do not stand alone. Each belief carries with it a set of other consequent beliefs. Or, more particularly, it rules out certain other beliefs. For example, imagine that my son tells me that he doesn't believe in birthdays anymore.

"Oh, that's a shame," I reply to him, "because that means that you won't be getting any cards or presents and you won't have a birthday party."

"No," he says, "I still want those. I still believe in birthday cards, birthday presents, and birthday parties. I just don't believe in birthdays anymore."

The fact is that he can't have it both ways. If he no longer believes in birthdays, he has automatically ruled out any other beliefs in the things that stem from them. In the same way, if people decide that they do not believe in the supernatural, then they have also automatically ruled out any other beliefs that depend upon the supernatural.

Second, any beliefs that we hold tend to have an effect on the way in which we behave. Beliefs even seem to act at an unconscious level. We may not have thought through the implications of a certain belief, nor even be aware that we actually hold that belief at all, and yet the belief does have an effect upon our actions.

Taking these two features of beliefs together, we can see that if we accept one particular belief, then it may mean that we have to abandon certain other beliefs, and whether we are aware of it or not, this may have a profound effect upon the way in which we behave.

We will now see how these two features help to explain why naturalism tends to lead to sexual promiscuity. A belief in naturalism rules out a belief in self-control. This is because in order to have self-control we must have free will, and if human beings are nothing but natural physical processes, then free will is one thing we cannot have.

When we lose our belief in the reality of self-control (whether we are consciously aware of it or not), this, in turn, takes the brakes off the biological, psychological, and sociological causes that drive us toward sexual activity. Thus it opens the floodgates to sexual promiscuity.

To consider this a bit more slowly, let's start with an illustration. Imagine a pool table with a set of balls on it. A player walks up to the table, takes his cue in his hand, and strikes the white ball. Now suppose that we were able to know every single physical feature about the table. Imagine we know exactly how hard the ball has been struck, in which direction, the precise position of each of the other balls, the friction of the table, the amount of bounce that each cushion provides, etc. If we had all that data, then it would be possible for us to predict exactly where each of the billiard balls would come to rest.

That is because the pool table is a purely physical system. The balls have no free will. They don't decide whether they want to move or not. They can't exercise any self-control and decide that they are not going to move once they have been struck. The whole process is determined as if it is controlled by a set of physical laws that act in a chain of cause-and-effect—and each effect is completely determined by its cause.

So much for pool tables. What about the rest of the world? If we believe in naturalism, then we find that we must believe that the whole world is like a massive, highly complex pool table where everything acts in a chain of cause-and-effect and all events are determined by previously existing natural causes. This logical extension of naturalism is sometimes called "determinism."

Pierre Laplace was an eighteenth-century French mathematician and philosopher who was a firm believer in
naturalism and determinism. He is best known for the
time when he demonstrated to the Emperor Napoleon
how Isaac Newton's mathematical calculations could
explain the irregularities in the movements of planets
without the need for a belief in any supernatural adjust-
ment. Napoleon asked him where God fit into his ideas.
Laplace replied, "I have no need of that hypothesis."

Furthermore, Laplace argued that, because everything
can be explained naturally and is determined physically, if
we were to know the exact position of everything in the
entire universe, then we would be able to predict everything that would happen throughout the whole universe
for the rest of eternity. According to Laplace, the whole
universe is like that pool table (but on a much larger
scale), where every cause has a predictable effect. So if
we know all the causes, we can exactly predict all the
effects.

But what about human free will? We are part of this
universe. Is Laplace saying that it would even be possible
to predict every thought, decision, and action that
humans make? The answer is yes. If we accept naturalism,
then we have to reject the concept of free will. If naturalism means that every part of this world can be explained
by natural processes, then that includes human brains.
And if every event in this world is determined, then that
also includes the events that take place in our brains—our
mental processes.

Will Provine, a biologist at Cornell University, has said,
"Humans are comprised only of heredity and environment,
both of which are deterministic. . . . From my perspective

as a naturalist, there's not even a possibility that human beings have free will."[14]

But what about our personal experience of free will? We don't think that every decision we make is just the effect of a particular set of causes; we experience a sense of freedom. We feel as if we have an ability to choose and to make decisions. But if naturalism is correct, then that experience is not real.

The psychologist Susan Blackmore has put it this way: "The idea that there is a self in there that decides things, acts and is responsible is a whopping great illusion. The self that we construct is just an illusion because actually there is only brains and chemicals and this 'self' doesn't exist."[15]

Similarly, Francis Crick, one of the scientists who unraveled the mystery of DNA, says that our sense of free will is only a feeling. He says that it isn't really true. We may feel that we have free will, but we don't really because "your sense of personal identity and free will are in fact no more than the behavior of a vast assembly of nerve cells and their associated molecules."[16]

This concept is very hard for people to accept. That is why most people don't think about it. Some, like Susan Blackmore and Francis Crick, have faced up to the implications of their belief in naturalism. Many others have not. They are happy to believe in naturalism, but only because they haven't realized that this necessarily cuts away any belief that they had in free will. Like my son, they want to reject the birthdays but keep the birthday presents.

Incidentally, there is a third set of people who realize the implications of naturalism but try to sidestep them with some crafty arguments. They try to say that it is possible to believe in naturalism and yet also believe in free will. They base their argument on the findings of scientists working in the field of quantum mechanics. Such scientists have shown that, although it is true that the world seems deterministic when we look at it on a large scale, when we look at it much more closely, we find that it actually appears to be indeterminate. To return to the pool table illustration, these scientists acknowledge that the movement of the balls seems deterministic but argue that if we were to look inside the balls, we would see a different picture.

There is no doubt that when scientists look inside atoms they do see a world that appears random and unpredictable. Albert Einstein argued that this must simply be due to the inadequacy of our current scientific knowledge. He proposed that there must be some hidden variable that, when discovered, will restore determinacy to the whole of physics. However, most scientists don't believe such a hidden variable exists and accept that the subatomic world is actually indeterminate. This has become known as the "Copenhagen interpretation" because its main promoter, Niels Bohr, worked in that city.

Consequently, some people have used this belief in indeterminacy in quantum mechanics in an attempt to believe in both naturalism and free will at the same time. If the subatomic world is not determinate, then could this allow us to have free will through purely natural processes? For instance, Roger Penrose, the Oxford mathematician, has argued that free will operates at the interface between the subatomic and atomic level in the brain. He has even proposed that it is located in the microtubules that can expand and shrink between the two levels.[17]

However, despite the attempts of Roger Penrose and others, one cannot use such arguments to reconcile naturalism and free will, because the indeterminacy of quantum mechanics is not consistent with free will. Free will is the ability to make a voluntary choice or decision, whereas the indeterminacy in quantum mechanics is due to randomness. This is something quite different. One could try to argue that our decision-making processes include elements of randomness along with determinacy. But one cannot argue that this constitutes free will as we understand it and experience it. Randomness is not compatible with voluntary choices or decisions.

Furthermore, they would do well to be cautious when they argue that something that seems random is in fact random. Advances in the branch of science known as "chaos theory" have shown that it is possible for events that appear to be random and chaotic actually to be governed by strictly deterministic laws. The events may not be predictable to us, because minute alterations in the cause bring about a great difference in the effect, but they are still deterministic.

So it seems inevitable that those who believe in naturalism must be forced to abandon any belief they might have held in free will. They can (cautiously) replace it with randomness instead of determinacy if they like, but it is still not free will.

## It's Not My Fault—Don't Blame Me!

At this point you may be wondering how many of today's teenagers are aware of such complex scientific and philosophical arguments. And how many, if they did know about them, would understand them anyway. The answer, of course, is not a lot. But, although they may not have heard of the terms nor understood the concepts, they still seem to have been affected by them. This is because of the way in which they have been taken into popular culture in recent years.

The philosophical belief systems of naturalism and determinism have been known in science for centuries. Throughout that time they seem to have had little effect upon the average person, and even less upon the average teenager. However, in the last few decades this has all changed.

Today's teenagers are the first generation to have grown up surrounded by such ideas because it is only in the last few decades that naturalism and determinism have been popularized in mainstream culture, largely through the publicity that has been given to the recent research in genetics.

In the middle of the 1980s scientists suggested that they should make a concerted attempt to map the human genome—the total genetic content of a human cell. Thus the Human Genome Project began, based at the new National Center for Human Genome Research, at the Institute of Health in Bethesda, Maryland. The Congress of the United States allocated some $3 billion to the project, which officially started on October 1, 1990, and is due to be completed in the year 2005. The goal is to map the sixty thousand to eighty thousand human genes in the human genome and to make them accessible for further biological study, as well as to determine the complete sequence of the 3 billion DNA subunits (bases).

On the one hand, the Human Genome Project is simply a scientific investigation. But, on the other hand, it seems to have been used to carry into popular culture the belief that scientists will soon be able to find genes that determine everything about us, including our behavior. Consequently, the popular media have been full of stories that researchers have identified genes that determine such behaviors as aggression, crime, depression, alcoholism, or anorexia. Newspapers frequently carry headlines such as "Scientists identify gene for depression" and "Aggression is determined by our genes" and "Official: lust is all in the genes." The substance is always much less dramatic and conclusive than the headline. But it is the headline that carries the message into popular culture.

As always, there is another side to the story. In the long tradition of the nature-nurture debate, there are those who respond by pointing out that our genes cannot, on their own, determine our behavior. For instance, when the report entitled "Genetics of Criminal and Anti-social Behavior" was published in 1996, Professor Sir Michael Rutter responded by saying, "Genes do not lead people directly to commit criminal acts. There may be an increased—in some cases greatly increased—propensity to aggression or anti-social behavior but whether or not the affected individual actually commits some criminal act will also be dependent upon environmental predisposing factors or situational circumstances at the time."[18]

Similarly, Professor Steve Jones responded to the research seeking to identify genes for higher IQ by saying, "Yes, it may be possible in the future to manipulate those genes. But it would be easier to change a population's IQ by doubling teachers' pay. Social engineering works more effectively."[19]

Notice that, whatever view such scientists express on

the nature-nurture debate, they still seem to hold to the naturalistic belief in determinism. They may argue that our behavior is determined by our genes or by our environment or by some combination of both, but none of them talks about free will, self-control, or individual responsibility. Thus determinism is popularized in mainstream culture. As with the story of the man stealing wheelbarrows that I told in the introduction, there may be heated debate about the content in terms of genes and environment—while the underlying wheelbarrow of determinism gets smuggled through into popular culture unquestioned.

Most teenagers may not be able to define naturalism or determinism, but they have grown up in a world in which those concepts have been popularized. Through this many of them have picked up the idea that their behavior is, in some way, determined by factors beyond their control.

At a time when they are spreading their wings, thinking for themselves, and developing their independence from their parents, today's teenagers are surrounded by a culture that has told them that their behavior is the result of their genes or their environment. We should not, therefore, be surprised when we hear them say, "Don't blame me," "It's not my fault," or "I can't help it."

If they have absorbed the idea that their behavior is determined and they have no real free will, can we then expect them to take responsibility for their actions or to exercise self-control? In recent years Western culture has been infused with the implicit assumption that nothing is really anyone's fault and we are quite powerless to change—we must just go with the flow.

The stand-up-comic-turned-writer Ben Elton has parodied this view brilliantly in his play and novel *Popcorn*. This is the story of Bruce, a film director who won't take responsibility for the effect of his films, and Wayne and Scout, two murderers who won't take responsibility for their crimes.

In a crucial scene, Bruce describes how he got off a drunk—driving charge by pleading that he had an addictive personality. He recounts, "That's what I said. Not 'I'm sorry your honor, I'm an irresponsible sh—t' but 'I can't help it. I have an addictive personality.' I drank the booze, I drove the car, but it wasn't my fault! I had a problem, you see, and it saved me from a prison term." He then refers to someone else who had been exposed as a serial adulterer. "He said he was addicted to sex. Not just a gutless, cheating little f—k-rat, you notice. No. A sex addict. He had a problem, so it was not his fault."[20]

Reflecting on contemporary society, Bruce says, "Nothing is anybody's fault. We don't do wrong, we have problems. We're victims, alcoholics, sexaholics. . . . Victims! . . . We are building a culture of gutless, spineless, self-righteous, whining cry-babies who have an excuse for everything and take responsibility for nothing."

I think Ben Elton has described modern culture very well. The chickens of naturalism and determinism have come home to roost. We have lost our confidence in free will. We have lost our belief in self-control. Consequently, we think we must "express ourselves" and "do what comes naturally" and "be true to ourselves."

So, if teenagers have had the source of their confidence in self-control taken away, what is there to stop them from giving free rein to the biological, psychological, and

sociological factors that drive them toward all sorts of
sexual activity? The brakes have been taken off and
thrown away.

"I just can't stop myself," said Liz, a seventeen-year-old
who looked strong, capable, and self-assured. "I don't
want to sleep around, and when I'm on my own, I decide
that I'm not going to do it again. But then I go out with a
boy, we go back to my room, and I know it's no good
trying to stop myself or him. I know I'll hate myself for it
afterwards but there's nothing I can do. It happens; it's
natural; it's just the way it is."

Such attitudes should make us very concerned. If the
loss of self-control is leading to teenage promiscuity
today, then where will it lead tomorrow? Self-control
limits not only our sexual activity but also a whole range
of other self-destructive and antisocial behaviors.

## Taking Back Control

How are we going to help teenagers rediscover their self-
control? How can we help them see that they are not at
the mercy of their genes, they are not governed by their
glands? How can we enable them to see that they can
help it, that they can change?

As in the case of teen obsession with appearance, we
could say that the answer lies in education, the home, or
the media. We could look for ways to teach and encourage self-control. We could find ways to give teenagers
more responsibility and hold them accountable for how
they exercise it. We could seek to encourage teenagers to
read books or watch films that highlight the value of
honor, patience, and self-control. We could find ways to
encourage them to go on Outward Bound courses or join
```
```

athletic teams, where they will learn that they can control their bodies, that they don't have to give up and take the easy route.

All of these practical attempts to help today's teenagers discover that they can exercise self-control, that they can be responsible, that they are not at the mercy of deterministic factors may be helpful. But once again they will struggle uphill against the powerful implicit message of naturalism that tells us that our behavior is determined by our genes and our environment.

Like a doctor trying to help a gravely ill person, we must do more than treat the symptoms; we must attempt to cure the disease itself. Aspirin will bring down the fever, but antibiotics are needed to eliminate the infection that causes the fever. When it comes to teen promiscuity, the loss of self-control is the "fever" and the naturalistic outlook on human nature is the "infection."

We already know that most teenagers believe in God. That is, they assent to the existence in some form of a Supreme Power. If you probed them, however, you'd quickly discover that few of them believe in the infinite-personal God of the Bible, creator and sustainer of the universe, who came to earth in the form of Jesus Christ. Rather, most have some rather vague idea of God as a loving being who is there if they want to call on Him and who doesn't expect too much of them. Thus these teens, while saying they believe in God, are practical atheists in the sense that they live as if God does not exist. They don't know Him and are not committed to Him.

In a situation like this we must do the slow, patient work of raising kids' understanding of who God is. As they learn to know what He's like—and even better, learn to know Him on a personal basis—they will begin to understand themselves better as well. They'll know that they are not just biological mechanisms who have no choice but to act on their urges. They'll realize that to be made in the image of God is a noble thing and that they are able to take charge of their own behavior.

Nature was made by God and is under the control of God. It is not autonomous. So understanding that God exists changes our perspective on nature, and especially our perspective on our favorite part of nature, namely, ourselves. We are not like the billiard balls—helpless to move unless we're acted upon. No matter what the Human Genome Project discovers, no matter where the nature-nurture debate goes, we can be sure that by God's grace we are able to make choices to do right and not wrong.

Surprisingly enough, some help in convincing kids that science has not explained everything and that God exists may come from science itself. Recent magazine articles have focused on how science has "found God." What they're saying is that scientific evidence in some fields is tending to support things that Christians have been saying all along. For instance, the evidence for the big bang keeps piling up, and yet science can give no explanation for why the big bang happened in the first place. A reasonable inference, even to an increasing number of scientists, seems to be that a Creator was behind it.

Whether or not science ever becomes a strong ally of Christian witness to God, we should not view science as the enemy. The enemy is naturalism, a system of belief that excludes God. Thus it's the interpretation and not the facts that we're disputing. It's the flaws in naturalism—and the incredibly sad consequences of it, if it's true—that we need to be exposing to our young people. And if science itself comes to our aid, sooner or later, in crumbling the foundations of naturalism, so much the better.

In my work I've seen teenagers come to a new understanding of God, and I've seen it change them forever. I've seen them take control of their lives, including their sexuality. And I've seen how teenagers who hated themselves for their promiscuity or who hated the hardness that had developed in their hearts begin to look at themselves with more respect. They have become better people, with more self-discipline in all areas of their lives, eventually making them better students, better employees, better wives and husbands, better mothers and fathers. But it all began with taking God seriously and understanding who He is.

And now it's time to look at one last behavior problem among today's teenagers. It's one that those who parent or teach teenagers will recognize all too well.

6

# "Shut Up, Granddad"
## *Understanding Teen Disrespect*

*"It's like being bitten to death by ducks."*
*—A mother tired of squabbling with her daughter*

*"Conflict, in the form of nagging, squabbling, and bickering,*
*is more common during adolescence*
*than during any other period of development."*
—Psychology Today *magazine[1]*

Bill was well into his seventies, but his mind was as sharp and clear as ever. He didn't like mysteries; he always wanted to figure them out and understand them. But there was one thing that he found he just could not fathom anymore. That was his fifteen-year-old grandson.

"I don't know what has happened to John," he said.

"We used to be so close, but not anymore. I remember the time when he seemed to think that I knew everything. If he had a problem, he wanted me to fix it. If I told him the best way to do something, he immediately believed me. I actually felt a bit embarrassed by the awe and respect in which he held me. But recently things have changed. He seems to think that I know nothing. He doesn't want my advice and certainly won't do anything I tell him. He just makes fun of me and tells me to shut up because I don't understand."

Bill was worried by John's new attitude toward him. Was he right to be so concerned? Is John's attitude really dangerous and disturbing? We might answer both yes and no.

Some of the changes that have taken place in John's attitude may be considered a normal, healthy part of growing up. As a young boy, John was dependent upon many people, including his granddad. But he cannot live his whole life in a dependent way—he must become independent. This is clearly vital. All children must learn to stand on their own two feet. It is during the teenage years that they make major steps forward in this progression from dependence to independence.

Such a progression has always happened, as long as human beings have lived on the earth. It has probably always been difficult and painful for children, parents, and grandparents alike as they have had to adjust to new relationships and positions.

However, what Bill described was something more than just this transition. John wasn't merely becoming independent of his grandfather; he also seemed to be rejecting him altogether. John didn't just decline his grandfather's advice; he also appeared to ridicule it. He seemed to treat his grandfather as if he knew nothing, as if he were useless. Obviously this worried Bill. I think he was right to be concerned.

As we talked together, I tried to help Bill understand some of the reasons why his grandson may have been behaving in this way, to see the underlying changes that have taken place in the attitude of many teenagers toward older people, and to see this in the context of a wider rejection, not just of age in particular, but of all authority.

Let's look at some of the cultural changes that Bill and I discussed. As we have found in the earlier chapters in this book, we will need to think quite widely and deeply. Let's start by looking back about five hundred years.

Johannes Gutenberg was a fifteenth-century German craftsman who loved to invent things. After spending many years and lots of money, he managed to design and build the first really effective printing press. He could not have realized at that time what an impact this was going to have upon the future of civilization.

Initially, printing was expensive and rather limited. But in time the printing presses of the world began to churn out masses of printed material. Today there are countless millions of books in print, everything from throwaway novels to huge encyclopedias. This has had a profound effect upon the place of elders and tradition in Western culture because the proliferation of printing has moved the main location of knowledge from the human brain to the printed page.

Before Gutenberg's invention, knowledge was mainly held by people. Some things were written down in manuscripts and laboriously copied for others, but not many. If

you wanted to discover some information, you would
have to ask someone who knew. For the vast majority of
people, there were no books that you could read or
libraries that you could visit. You had to rely upon the
knowledge held by others.

In most cases the people who held the knowledge were
older people. They had lived the longest and so had been
able to accumulate the most information. They had
learned it from their elders, who in turn had received it
from their elders—and they knew that this chain went
back in time through a rich family and tribal tradition that
was highly respected.

It is not surprising, then, that older people were held in
high regard. They were crucial for the development of
younger people. And the traditions through which
younger people learned from older people were vital to
the survival of the culture. This meant that history was
important to everyone, both young and old. They knew
that they were not the only generation that had ever
mattered. They were dependent on their elders and their
traditions. Their heritage was vitally important to them.

There are some parts of the world today where this still
applies. There are cultures that we sometimes (rather
patronizingly) call primitive and that have no printed, or
perhaps even written, material. In these communities
knowledge is still held by older people. It is significant
that in such cultures ancestors, living elders, and tribal
traditions are still held in high regard. They are vital to the
storage and transmission of knowledge and the survival
of the culture.

However, printing tends to change this. The printing
press makes knowledge available to everyone, regardless

of their relationship to older people or their experience of tribal traditions. In the West, for instance, we are surrounded by books. There are libraries full of them. Many people have scores, if not hundreds, of them in their own home. So, if people want to find out some information, they can look it up in a book or read it in a newspaper or a magazine. They no longer need an older person.

Similarly, our education system centers upon books and not upon elders and traditions. Our young people do not learn through sitting around the campfire listening to old people telling the traditional tribal stories. They learn at school, using books. Thus old people (and particularly old family members) are removed from the educational process. And so it is not surprising that old people are no longer held in high regard.

But why is it that the effects of this change seem to have become apparent only in recent years? If the printing press was invented five hundred years ago, why have the consequences taken so long to come about? Clearly there are other factors at work here.

To some extent, it seems that the full effect of the printing press was delayed until widespread schooling developed. It is only in the twentieth century that all young people have received a long, book-based education. Previously, despite the existence of the printing press, many young people still learned a trade through a period of apprenticeship to older people.

To a greater extent, the effect of the printing press seems to have increased in the second half of the century, as it was multiplied by a growth on the amount of knowledge available. Take the world of science, for example, and consider how much has been discovered in the last fifty years. Thus any knowledge that an older person holds seems ever smaller compared to the total knowledge available in books. Furthermore, the knowledge they do have may now be out-of-date. Granddad may have learned about Newton's laws of physics, but how much does he know about cryogenics, the anthropic principle, or artificial intelligence?

But those two factors do not explain the great changes in recent decades. Another, newer factor must be added to the printing press effect—the invention of personal computers and the Internet.

The printing press moved the location of knowledge from the elders' brains to the book. But books were equally accessible to old and young alike. The technological revolution of recent decades has taken knowledge on to computers, which tend to be less accessible to many older people.

Computers have opened up possibilities for information storage and retrieval that could not have been imagined a generation ago. I myself have a copy of the *Encyclopedia Britannica* on a single CD-ROM, and another CD that contains the text of over 3,500 of the world's classic literary works, from Hippocrates through Shakespeare to Mark Twain.

In turn, computers have opened the door to the Internet. For a few dollars each month, it is possible to access information from computers all around the world. Whatever your area of interest, you can obtain apparently limitless amounts of knowledge at the click of a mouse.

Today's teenagers are the first generation to have grown up surrounded by such technology. Many of them spend large amounts of time with their fingers on a keyboard and their eyes on a screen. For this reason, Douglas Rushkoff has given a new name to these teenagers: he calls them "screenagers."[2]

Thus, while teenagers are able to access this newly available wealth of knowledge, many elderly people are not. Computer skills are picked up quite easily by teenagers and even by those much younger. But older people typically find it much harder. Many elderly people don't want to touch a computer at all.

Is this the reason why many teenagers seem to regard older people as an embarrassing irrelevance, well past their sell—by date? It clearly explains a lot. But there are also some other issues we need to consider.

## Knowledge or Wisdom?

The rejection of older people through the development of printing, computers, and the Internet has been possible only because knowledge has become much more highly valued than wisdom. If we are to find a solution to the problem of many teenagers' views of older people, it is vital that we understand the difference between these two concepts.

"Knowledge" can be defined as a body of truth or information that has been acquired. These facts or data can be held by a person or in a book or on a computer. Wisdom is quite different. This is the ability to discern; it involves inner qualities and good sense. It cannot be contained in a book or on a computer but only in a person.

It is true that there are books that we might be tempted to think contain wisdom, such as the ancient Egyptian *Instruction of Amenemope*, some of the Mesopotamian writings, and the Book of Proverbs in the Bible. However, despite the fact that these are often called "wisdom literature," they are not wisdom. They are wise sayings. Even if one had a library full of such wise sayings, or logged on to a database on which they were all indexed, one would not have wisdom. The essential characteristic of wisdom is the ability to discern. This cannot be written down or encoded on a computer disk. Wisdom is not a piece of abstract information; it is a feature of a human being. One cannot *have* wisdom in the sense that one can have a set of information or a piece of knowledge; one *is* wise.

Wisdom, then, is hard to attain. It takes time. It cannot be accessed immediately or downloaded from a Web site. In recent years, with the phenomenal growth of knowledge and with the desire for instant access, it is not surprising that our culture has come to value knowledge above wisdom.

Some saw this coming. Martin Luther King Jr. put it this way: "Our scientific power has outrun our spiritual power. We have guided missiles and misguided men." Similarly, Winston Churchill said, "We know how to control everything except man himself."

Many teenagers today also recognize an emptiness in knowledge without wisdom. They have found that, no matter how much they learn at school or college, this doesn't seem to help them with the big issues of life. I remember one biology student putting this very clearly when he said, "My course tells me how I live—but not what I should live for." If we can help teenagers find this wisdom, then perhaps they would have answers to their big questions. And also, almost as a by-product, they would once more see the immense value in older people.

But wisdom brings with it authority. So, if they are to find wisdom, they must be prepared to accept authority. And here we face another problem.

In recent years many teenagers have rejected not only older people in particular but also authority in general. Teachers are not usually respected simply because they are teachers. They need to work hard to earn the respect that they once had by right. The police have a similar problem.

So why are we facing this crisis of authority? Why do so many teenagers seem to reject any form of authority? To understand this, we need to look at some etymology as well as some political history and philosophy.

The word "authority" is derived from the word "author." Thus, in the original meaning of the term, the concept of authority derived from the concept of an author. If an author has created something, she necessarily has rights over that which owes its very existence to her—she has authority over it. She may give that authority to someone else, but that authority is only worth anything because it comes from her, the creator.

If we look back in history, we find that civilizations have always derived their concept of authority from a belief in a Creator God. That God is the ultimate author and therefore the ultimate source of all authority. God may then give individual authority to people on earth— whether grandparents or parents, teachers or kings—but that authority is only worth anything because it comes from the Creator.

For example, in ancient China rulers were thought to have the *"T'ien Ming"*—the mandate of heaven. This Chinese Confucian idea had its beginnings in the early

Chou dynasty, about 1000 B.C. The Chinese believed that
heaven gave the right to rule directly to an emperor, who
was seen as the Son of Heaven.

Many centuries later, in the Byzantine Empire around
the eastern Mediterranean, the concept known as
caesaropapism was developed. This was a system
whereby the emperor was recognized as the head of both
the church and the state. The Byzantines believed that, in
both these roles, he derived his authority from God.

The idea was later formulated into the belief in the
"divine right of kings" by people such as the French
bishop Jacques Bossuet and the English squire Sir Robert
Filmer. The divine right of kings was based upon the view
that kings derive their authority directly from God.
Unfortunately, it was also extended to the belief that,
because of the source of their authority, they could not be
held accountable for their actions to any earthly authority,
such as a parliament. Of course this led to abuses.
Therefore, it was rejected by philosophers such as John
Locke (with his *First Treatise of Civil Government* in 1689)
and it was fought against in the English Civil War, the
French Revolution, and the American War of
Independence.

However, these struggles were not fought against the
concept of a Creator God who gives authority but
against the regal misuse of that concept. For instance,
the classic rejection of the authority of kings, the
American Declaration of Independence, says that
governments "derive their just power from the consent
of the governed" but that this, in turn, comes from the
fact that "they are endowed by their Creator with
certain unalienable rights." So, even though the king's

authority was rejected, the people still believed that authority is ultimately derived from God.

In the years since then, however, God Himself has been largely rejected by Western culture, as we have seen in earlier chapters of this book. But if a culture has declared that God is dead, what then happens to authority? If a belief in authority is derived from a belief in an author, what happens when people no longer believe that there is an author?

The French atheistic philosopher Jean-Paul Sartre gave a clear answer to these questions in his famous lecture entitled "Existentialism and Humanism," which he delivered in Paris in 1944. In this he said, "God does not exist and we have to face all the consequences of this. . . . It is extremely embarrassing that God does not exist, for there disappears with him all possibility of finding values in an intelligible heaven. . . . We find no values or commands to turn to."

Quite right. If there is no God, then there is no ultimate author and so there is no ultimate authority. We must make up our own mind about right and wrong, truth and error. Thus there are no absolutes; everything depends upon the individual. Individuals may join together and make a "social contract" on the basis of an agreed consensus, but this may be different for different peoples at different times—so there is still no ultimate basis for authority.

This position is usually referred to as "relativism." Relativism says that there is no absolute truth and no absolute right or wrong. Everything depends upon who you are, where you are, what you are, when you are.

Relativism was perhaps most clearly expressed by the

Cambridge scholar Don Cupitt: "Capital T truth is dead. . . . Truth is plural, socially conditioned and perpetually changing." It is more commonly revealed in statements such as "That's OK for you, but it's not for me" or "That may be true for you, but it is not true for me."

Once again, today's teenagers are the first generation to have grown up in a culture that is steeped in relativism. Within a few decades of Sartre's lecture we find that most teenagers seem to agree with him. This is so even among church-attending teenagers. In a survey of teens who identify themselves as born again, six out of ten said there is no such thing as absolute truth. Even more remarkably, nine out of ten say that right and wrong depend on the individual and situation—moral relativism.[3]

This loss of absolute truth and absolute right and wrong is bound to have consequences for society. Sartre, in his lecture, quoted the Russian novelist Dostoyevsky, who said, "Everything is permissible if God does not exist." Correct. If there is no God, then we cannot really talk about anything being wrong. Nothing can be absolutely wrong. It is just wrong for us, in our culture, at our time, if we decide it is wrong.

I work with teenagers day by day, helping them to explore spiritual and moral issues. Until a few years ago I had never met a completely relativist teenager. When they thought about it, they all believed that some things were absolutely wrong. If I asked them whether rape or child abuse is wrong, they would tell me, "Of course it is." They believed these are wrong, not just because we choose to say that they are, but because they are. They didn't always know why, but they believed these things are absolutely wrong.

However, in my experience, this has begun to change very fast in the past few years. I now meet increasing numbers of teenagers who are quite convinced that nothing is absolutely wrong. Just a few days before writing this, I led a conference for 120 teenagers, of whom about ten argued vigorously with me that nothing, not even child abuse or rape, is absolutely wrong. "Morality," they said, "is decided by consensus. Things are only right or wrong if we decide that they are—so nothing can be absolutely wrong."

This may shock us, but it should not be surprising. If our culture has rejected God, is it not inevitable that people will reject authority? If there is no God to give any ultimate authority, if everything is relative and we must all make up our own minds, why should anyone accept anyone else's authority?

You may decide that something is right, but I may have a different view. Who is to say that you are right and I am wrong? So what if you happen to be a police officer, a teacher, or a judge—or even any older person? Why is your view any better than mine just because you are older or hold a particular position? Why should you have any authority over me?

Thus there is a tendency among today's teenagers to lose their concept of authority along with their appreciation of the value of wisdom, their family, their national heritage, and older people. Such a conclusion may lead us to think that those of us who are older will never be able to relate properly to teenagers, let alone help them. Even if we have understood all the reasons underlying each aspect of the behavior that we have considered in this book, it would seem that there is nothing that we can do about it—because they are not going to listen to us anyway.

It is clearly true that we cannot just tell them what to do. But are there ways in which we can help them—as individuals and as a society? I believe there are.

## Restoring Authority

To sum up, older people have become marginalized because of the way in which our culture prizes knowledge above wisdom. And we have lost confidence in the notion of authority because of our rejection of the concept of an Author, and the consequent relativization of truth and morals.

So how are we going to help today's teenagers to deal with this? Yet again we could say that the answer lies in education, the home, or the media. We could look for ways to teach our teenagers about the value of older people. We could find older people with skills and abilities that our teenagers need (such as the ability to fix their car or improve their football skills) and put them together. We could find old people with interesting personal stories to tell, whom our teenagers could interview for their history projects. We could organize or enter competitions that require older and younger people to pool their knowledge to succeed. We could ask our teenagers to use their computers to draw up and record the family tree.

All of these practical attempts to help today's teenagers to discover the value of their heritage and their place in history may be helpful. But they will struggle uphill against the powerful implicit message that stems from the rejection of wisdom and authority, and the consequent moral relativism. We must deal with this.

First, we must recognize that relativism is founded upon

an underlying cultural rejection of God. If there is no God, then there are no moral absolutes. However, if God does exist, then the picture changes radically.

Second, we must recognize that ideas and information all carry with them a deeper message. Whatever is taught explicitly in schools, in homes, or in the media carries with it certain beliefs and values. For instance, ideas about the right to rule, which are taught in history, bring with them a set of consequent beliefs and values about the nature of authority.

If we are concerned about teenagers, we must make sure that what is taught is true and that the implicit beliefs and values that are carried with it are brought into the open. Let's look at this in relation to schools (but recognizing that the need for consistency we will discover is just as relevant in the home and in the media).

If it truly is the case that God does not exist and that there is no ultimate authority, then we must learn to live with the implications of this. That means that we should help our schools to teach this consistently throughout the curriculum. We may find that we have to rewrite most of the current school mission statements. How can a school declare that its pupils must value individuals for who they are, take responsibility for their actions, and have respect for authority if these beliefs are fundamentally without foundation?

On the other hand, if God does exist and we are created in His image, with intrinsic value, worth, freedom, and authority, then, again, we must learn to live with the implications of this. The school mission statement described above would be perfectly valid, but we would need to think carefully about the implicit beliefs and values communicated by the curriculum subjects as they are currently taught.

The problem is that in many schools young people are given two conflicting messages. The school mission statement may tell them that everyone is valuable, that everyone should exercise self-control and respect authority. But in biology they may learn that we have evolved through death of the least fit; in psychology they may learn that our behavior is determined by our genes and environment; in history they may learn that authority is tyranny that should be rejected.

So, where do we go from here? If we recognize that we do need to be consistent one way or the other, which way should we go? How can we decide? Clearly, we are driven to that fundamental question: does God exist? It seems that belief in God cannot be simply an issue for individuals. There are many beliefs that individuals hold that are personal and private. Whether or not I believe that the Chicago Cubs are a great team to support is really just a private belief for me on my own. However, God's existence is a public rather than a private issue, for it has implications for the whole of our culture.

Nietzsche, whom we have met several times in this book, severely criticized people who rejected God but held on to traditional beliefs and values that derive from God. This is one of the few points on which I agree with him. If God does not exist, let's be consistent and, as a culture, not try to hold on to past beliefs and values that stem from Him. However, if we look at the lives of many of today's teenagers and begin to see how devastating it has been to let go of those beliefs and values, does that not motivate us to consider seriously whether, in fact,

God may actually exist? If we find that He does exist after all, then we will know that those beliefs and values that we so desperately need to rediscover as a culture are actually well founded.

When we look at the behavior of some teenagers and ask the question "Why do they do that?" we find that many of the most powerful fundamental answers seem to be rooted in the philosophical rejection of God that underlies many of the changes in Western culture. Therefore, the existence or nonexistence of God cannot be just a matter for personal, private belief. It has such massive cultural implications, which we can see ultimately play out in the lives of today's teenagers, that we must consider the question not just as individuals but also as a culture, as a nation, as a community.

# Conclusion

I wrapped up each chapter in this book with an attempt to suggest how to respond to the problem addressed in the chapter. I believe those concluding parts of the chapter are the most important ones in the book—not for today's teenagers but for tomorrow's. Teenagers are not going to die out with this generation. No matter how much we are or are not able to help today's teenagers, we must recognize that there will be another generation of teenagers to come, and then another and another. If the culture in which we currently live has led to problems for today's teenager, then we must try to change it—for the sake of the next generation.

In the introduction I quoted from the writings of the American social commentator Douglas Rushkoff. When Rushkoff looks at the massive changes that have taken place in Western culture, he says, "Without having migrated an inch we have nonetheless traveled further than any generation in history."[1] He goes on to liken us to new immigrants in a new land: we are puzzled and perplexed by the strange world around us. He then argues that, if we are to settle into this new land, we must do what immigrants usually do—that is, follow our children. Since immigrants' children always lead the way in adapting to their new home, he argues that we should follow the attitudes, beliefs, and values of today's "children of chaos." He says, "Chaos is their natural environment. By following our screenagers' example rather than panicking at their embrace of turbulence, we may just stand a chance of adapting to the culture to which we are inevitably migrating."

Is this correct? I find myself agreeing with his analysis but disagreeing with his prescription. For there is another way of looking at the situation we face. Suppose I am an immigrant in a new land and I see my children adapting to their new home in ways that are deeply damaging to them and to others. What would I do? Rather than following their lead in settling down, I would try to change the land so that it will not harm the children of future generations.

That, I believe, is the situation we currently face in Western culture. Day by day I look at teenagers who are being profoundly damaged by the new world in which they live. And so I want to see that culture changed—for the teenagers of tomorrow. May God bless us as we work together for that aim.

# Notes

## Introduction

1. Douglas Rushkoff, *Children of Chaos* (New York: HarperCollins, 1997).

## Chapter 1/"All You Ever Do Is Criticize"

1. "Cathy" is not her real name. I will give false names to almost all the people whose stories I tell in this book. That is partly to protect their identity and partly so that people will still talk to me in the future without fear of being identified in a book! Indeed, some of the individual stories I tell through the book are compilations of a number of different people and situations.

2. R. S. Peters, *Education and the Education of Teachers* (London: Routledge, 1977).

3. In the fifth century B.C. the philosopher Socrates taught through asking a series of questions; this is now usually called the Socratic method.

4. Of course "postmodernism" is an inadequate name. It is also a misleading one, since postmodernism is not really an "-ism" at all. It isn't a coherent set of beliefs that constitute a complete metanarrative. In fact, it is based upon the rejection of coherent sets of beliefs and the abandonment of a search for a complete metanarrative. Therefore, it is better described as "postmodernity" rather than "postmodernism."

5. A metanarrative is an overall way of understanding the world.

Marxism is a metanarrative; so are Islam and Christianity, since they each claim to give a big story that explains the whole world.

6. *Jean Baudrillard: Selected Writings*, ed. Mark Poster (Stanford, Calif.: Stanford University Press, 1988).

7. So I understand from those who have watched it—I have not and don't intend to.

8. Rushkoff, *Children of Chaos*.

9. D. Boulton, *Sea of Faith* 16, January 1994.

## Chapter 2/Dancing with Death

1. Joyce Buchanan, "Monitoring the Future Study Press Release," December 18, 1998. Retrieved January 15, 1999, from the World Wide Web: http://www.isr.umich.edu/src/mtf/.

2. Charles Bowden, "Bad Luck on an Otherwise Fine Night," *Esquire*, March 1998, 78.

3. Deborah Padgett Barr, "My Daughter's Silent Agony," *McCall's*, November 1997, 93.

4. Buchanan, "Monitoring the Future."

5. "Monitoring the Future Study" (1998), Table 1a. Retrieved January 15, 1999 from the World Wide Web: http://www.isr.umich.edu/src/mtf/.

6. Joseph A. Califano Jr. and Alyse Booth, "1998 CASA National Survey of Teens, Teachers, and Principals." Retrieved January 15, 1999 from the World Wide Web: http://www.casacolumbia.org.

7. Bowden, "Bad Luck," 78.

8. See Plato's *Republic*.

9. Survey by The National Center on Addiction and Substance Abuse at Columbia University, 1996.

10. *Times* (London), October 23, 1996.

11. Survey by The National Center on Addiction and Substance Abuse at Columbia University, 1996.

12. To be more precise, they cited boredom and stress. Clearly teenagers face stress about many issues: exams, employment prospects, their image, their relationships, their developing sexuality. We will look at some of these stress factors in other chapters, but here I want to concentrate on the boredom aspect.

13. *New Internationalist*, July 1997.

14. Irvine Welsh, *Trainspotting* (London: Minerva, 1994).

15. *Statistical Abstract of the United States 1997*, 177th ed. (Lanham, Md.: Bernan, 1997), p. 57.

16. Bruce A. Chadwick and Tim B. Heaton, *Statistical Handbook on Adolescents in America* (Phoenix, Ariz.: Oryz, 1996), p. 12.

17. *Statistical Abstract*, p. 66.

18. Michel Maffesoli, "Jeux de masques," in *Design Issues IV*, 1988.

19. Zygmunt Bauman, *Intimations of Postmodernity* (London: Routledge, 1992).

## Chapter 3/"I Feel Like Giving Up"

1. Elizabeth Wurtzel, *Prozac Nation: Young and Depressed in America* (Boston: Houghton Mifflin, 1994).

2. *Statistical Abstract*, p. 103.

3. *Times Educational Supplement* (London), March 24, 1989.

4. Ibid.

5. Leslie Francis and William Kray, *Teenage Religion and Values* (Harrisburg, Pa.: Morehouse, 1995).

6. *The Gallup Survey on Teenage Suicide* (Princeton, N.J.: George H. Gallup International Institute, 1991), p. 75.

7. Quoted in Mark Williams, *Cry of Pain: Understanding Suicide and Self-Harm* (London: Penguin, 1997).

## Chapter 4/Fitting the Image

1. Tod Olson, "Images of Women: Should We All Be Like Kate?" *Scholastic Update*, March 8, 1996, p. 11.

2. Joan Jacobs Brumberg, *The Body Project: An Intimate History of American Girls* (New York: Random House, 1997).

3. David M. Garner, "The 1997 Body Image Survey Results," *Psychology Today*, January–February 1997, p. 30.

4. *Times* (London), June 3, 1996.

5. Caroline Woodroffe et al., *Children, Teenagers, and Health: The Key Data* (Buckingham: Open University Press, 1993).

6. Augustine, *Confessions.*

7. Times (London), September 8, 1997.

8. *The Religious Life of Young Americans* (Princeton, N.J.: George H. Gallup International Institute, 1992), p. 28.

9. George Barna, *Generation Next* (Ventura, Calif.: Regal, 1995), p. 103.

10. Desmond Morris, *Naked Ape: A Zoologist's Study of the Human*

*Animal* (New York: McGraw-Hill, 1967).

11. Francis Crick, *The Astonishing Hypothesis: Scientific Search for the Soul* (New York: Scribner's, 1994).

12. Others, such as Stephen Jay Gould, think that "meme" is a meaningless metaphor.

13. *The Skeptic*, May 1993.

14. Susan Blackmore, "Minds, Memes, and Selves," lecture given at the London School of Economics, November 28, 1996.

15. Richard Dawkins, *Climbing Mount Improbable* (New York: Norton, 1996).

16. Richard Dawkins, "Why We Exist," public lecture, London, April 25, 1996.

## Chapter 5/Just Do It

1. The Alan Guttmacher Institute, "Facts in Brief: Teen Sex and Pregnancy." Retrieved January 15, 1999, from the World Wide Web: http://www.agi-usa.org.

2. *Statistical Abstract*, p. 86.

3. P. L. Benson, *The Troubled Journey: A Portrait of 6th-12th Grade Youth* (Minneapolis: Search Institute, 1990), p. 54.

4. *Sex and America's Teenagers* (New York: Alan Guttmacher Institute, 1994), p. 29.

5. Guttmacher Institute, "Teen Sex."

6. Ibid.

7. The Alan Guttmacher Institute, "Special Report: U.S. Teenage Pregnancy Statistics." Retrieved January 15, 1999, from the World Wide Web: http://www.agi-usa.org.

8. Nicholas Humphries, *Soul Searching* (Chatto & Windus, 1995).

9. Friedrich Nietzsche, *Thus Spake Zarathustra*, trans. R. Hollingdale (New York: Penguin, 1961).

10. Carl Sagan, *The Demon-Haunted World: Science as a Candle in the Dark* (New York: Random House, 1996).

11. Barna, *Generation Next*, p. 103.

12. Gallup, *Religious Life*, p. 23

13. Ibid., p. 33

14. Russell Stannard, *Science and Wonders* (London: Faber & Faber, 1996).

15. *The Skeptic*, May 1993.

16. Crick, *Astonishing Hypothesis*.

17. See Roger Penrose, *The Emperor's New Mind: Concerning Computers, Minds, and the Laws of Physics* (New York: Oxford University Press, 1989); and *Shadows of the Mind: On Consciousness, Computation, and the New Physics* (New York: Oxford University Press, 1994).

18. Times (London), January 24, 1996.

19. Times (London), May 12, 1996.

20. Ben Elton, *Popcorn* (New York: Simon & Schuster, 1996), pp. 82–83.

## Chapter 6/"Shut Up, Granddad"

1. Laurance Steinberg, "Bound to Bicker," *Psychology Today*, September 1987, p. 36.

2. Rushkoff, *Children of Chaos.*

3. Barna, *Generation Next*, p. 104.

## Conclusion

1. Rushkoff, *Children of Chaos.*